THE DST REVOLUTION

1031 EXCHANGE INTO RETIREMENT MODE

DST AND PHILANTHROPY

THE DST REVOLUTION

1031 EXCHANGE INTO RETIREMENT MODE

DST AND PHILANTHROPY

2ND EDITION

DON MEREDITH
DST PIONEER

WITH

THOMAS KOSS
COMMERCIAL REAL ESTATE BROKER

THE DST REVOLUTION

Printed in the United States of America.

ISBN: 978-0-57864310-6 (paperback)
ISBN: 978-0-578-64311-3 (e-book)
Library of Congress Control Number: 2020902148

ACKNOWLEDGMENTS

I wish to thank first, my wife Brenda for endless hours editing etc., despite her full-time responsibilities at General Dynamics NASSCO.

I need to thank Charles Jensen from Inland Realty Group for his guidance and support early on in this project. For chasing down the founders to arrange interviews. Including a conference call to the founders, who happened to be in a limo with the NAR president from Illinois outside the gate of the White House waiting for a meeting with the Vice President.

A big thank you to Geoff Flahardy, one of the early pioneers and rocks of this industry!

I have to thank James Benes, Mr. Chicago, formerly CBS NewsRadio forty-years, for his guidance and editing and his great interviews with the founders and president of Inland.

And lastly, I'd like to give a special thanks to former PricewaterhouseCooper corporate auditor & CPA,

Mark Kosanke. Mark is the original pioneer and voice of the DST industry, and he is 14 years Alternative and Direct Investment Securities Association (ADISA) board member and former president.

TABLE OF CONTENTS

Revolution for Income Property Investors 9

How Does a Delaware Statutory Trust (DST) Work? 27

The Strength of a DST Solution 37

Untapped Wealth for Philanthropy 45

Getting Started 57

The Foundation, Trust and Integrity of this Industry Started with Inland 69

Interview with Keith Lampi, President & CEO 85

Interview with Warren Thomas, Founding Partner ExchangeRight 99

Cantor Fitzgerald 105

Accommodator's Perspective, your 1031 Exchange Escrow: Interview with William Exeter, President & CEO Exeter 1031 Exchange Service 107

Q&A with the Leading DST Money Guy: Conversation with Charles Jensen 117

"Voice of the Industry" Mark Kosanke 127

Should I buy my own NNN or a DST? 149

About the Author 151

REVOLUTION FOR INCOME PROPERTY INVESTORS

"**O**wning an apartment complex straddles the line between an investment and a career." So wrote Steve Lander on Chron.com. What is the value of your time? Can you put a value on time?

For many income property investors approaching or at retirement, the career part of that equation may no longer be as appealing. Here's where I need you to listen very carefully. If you knew what I know about Delaware Statutory Trusts (DSTs), you likely would be immediately putting them on the table as one of the most viable options to consider utilizing as an exit strategy.

The benefits to you could be many, not the least of which is no more tenants to deal with which translates to an improved quality of life for you. A few obvious questions should be asked before you move ahead with any exit strategy:

1) What is important to you?
2) Is it income replacement / preservation?
3) Do you want to donate money to your favorite charity?
4) Do you want to provide income and assets to your beneficiaries?
5) Would you like a method that will make it a little easier to strive toward those goals, resulting in minimal inconvenience and/or uncertainty?
6) Exactly what is the desired outcome you want?
7) And given all of this, what is the optimal strategy for you and how do you find out what that is?

The ultimate exit strategy is that we all pass on. Most people will leave their estate, their things of economic value, in a Trust created to divest those assets to heirs and others that are named as the beneficiaries of the trust. A designated Trustee will administer and oversee the assets on behalf of the beneficiaries as directed in the trust documentation.

But what will the Trustee's responsibilities be? Will the responsibilities be straight forward and easy to comply with or will they be complicated and difficult to perform? Will you be creating involuntary owners by leaving your beneficiaries properties that they really don't want, or don't really have the skill set or desire to manage? (Does that sound familiar?)

More often than not, when you leave investment properties to someone who does not want to own them all they will want to do is sell the property as quickly as possible. It can wind up as a de facto "fire sale" with asking prices often well below fair market value. In this instance the true value that you wish to pass along is discounted, something most people do not want to see happening.

And what if your beneficiaries don't get along and they wind up with ownership interests in the same property? That scenario can easily result in acrimonious communications that could then lead to lengthy and expensive litigation, all just to settle your estate. This undesirable scenario can easily be avoided.

There are a host of financial advisers, real estate agents, insurance people, and attorneys that may approach you with what they think are your most viable options. The more ethical ones will be aware that there are a number of options to consider and they will do their best to guide you to the ones most suited to meet your needs. The not so ethical ones will use honed sales skills to steer you towards options that benefit them first and you second.

In choosing the right advisor it is important to carefully check them out, do your homework and make sure you find one that works for you and has utmost integrity. As for me? I have been working with investment property owners for twenty-plus years and am always seeking the best options and solutions for the investors I work with. It has to be that way for me.

Part of what fuels my passion for what I do is that I have been awed and amazed repeatedly by the tenacity, the innovation, the self-reliance and the courage investors show in doing what they do. I have learned from them and have been honored to collaborate with them.

The investment property "Owner-Warrior" (that's the right term) continually demonstrates over time what good old-fashioned hard work and patience does in terms of accumulating real wealth. It works! Investing in assets that tend to appreciate and at the same time generate income? What a concept!

So why ever sell any property? Many investors can make a good case by the numbers for owning property forever and never selling. Those investors in the commercial real estate world are called "Hold and Die" owners. But the fact is that we all get older and most of us have retirement goals, travel plans and the like. Often times there may be health issues to consider as well. Living longer and more active lives than their parents, many baby-boomers find they need hip and knee replacements. Or sometimes life circumstances just change.

So, you're older now and your real estate has appreciated significantly in value. That factored in with some of those possible life changes mentioned above may make you think that now is the time to pull the trigger, sell your property, and put that equity to work without having to be involved in the day-to-day obligations of property ownership. Resolved: It is time to fully immerse into retirement mode and sell those properties.

Good News: one of the great things about DSTs is that you can defer any tax consequences via a 1031 Tax Deferred Exchange, and DSTs generate income. That's right, immediately. And there's flexibility on where that income goes. You decide whether it will be for your retirement needs, or whether you want to re-direct some or all of the income to a charity, to your beneficiaries, or to whatever.

DSTs afford you the flexibility to direct that income flow just about any way you want to. And you can make changes any time you want to. It is important to remember that although income is generated to the investors the entity itself that you are investing in is considered illiquid. The Trust (DST) has as the primary asset real estate. Typical life cycles I see in DSTs (formation to dissolution, also known as "going full cycle") is around 5-7 years, but they are designed to be long term, like 10 years, selling based on market conditions.

If you were to die sometime during the cycle, your beneficiaries would immediately get a step up in cost basis thus eliminating taxes that would have to have been paid were you to outright sell your property and not elected to exchange. The DST option also means it will likely be a few years before your trust gets these funds as a lump sum. But in the meantime, they would receive any income generated on a monthly basis through the holding period.

But back to the lifestyle benefits. What would life be like if you cleared the table of any responsibilities of active management? As one who became an oil painter and stage actor later in life, I can tell you there is life other than work! A 1031 tax deferred exchange into a

DST can deliver you there in a New York minute. [For a thorough definition of a 1031 Tax Deferred Exchange, jump to the chapter "Accommodators Perspective" with William Exeter.]

For some, the constant drumbeat for repairs, complaints about neighbors, concerns about capital maintenance, even frivolous litigations can take their toll over the years. For others the idea of selling properties they have known for years is like saying goodbye to a close family member. Realistically perhaps, they are no longer as enthusiastic about owning and managing the property as they once were.

Is there an exit strategy that makes sense? A strategy that I can get my hands around? Can I fully utilize the equity I have accumulated and deploy it to maximize monthly income? Have we considered the tax ramifications of just simply cashing out and investing the funds in a number of other ways, stocks, bonds etc.

Much has been written about the Delaware Statutory Trust as a 1031 Exchange. And for our readers who are attorneys and CPA's, yes please note 2004-86 IRS Revenue ruling. Now let me direct you to an article posted by one of the largest 1031 escrow companies in the country about DSTs. Why? Because there's a lot I can say about DSTs and will (as well as others) as the book continues, but I wanted you to hear from a completely independent source.

IPX Investment Property 1031 Exchange Services, Inc: A Subsidiary of Fidelity National Financial, a Fortune 500 Company. IPX wrote a detailed blog on their web site, "DSTs, an option to keep on your 1031 radar." This struck me as quite significant, as typically IPX doesn't often wander this close to endorsing any particular strategy from a specific industry. Considering all the research that a large institution puts into their content, I thought the endorsement signaled that DSTs had moved from what was a cottage industry to a multi-billion-dollar industry.

Let me share some of what was posted:

> "DSTs offer an intriguing option for investors who are looking for properties to complete their 1031 Exchanges.
>
> A DST (Delaware Statutory Trust) is an "arm chair investment", or a passive investment opportunity that allows individuals to own fractional shares in institutional grade properties. A DST is a legal entity created as a trust under Delaware law that can hold real estate. In the context of real estate, DSTs are formed pursuant to private governing agreements under which a

property or several properties are held, managed, administered, and/or operated for profit by a trustee for the benefit of the holders of the DSTs beneficial interests. Some examples of properties that were recently structured as DSTs are:

1. A portfolio of 17 storage properties in three states
2. An office building in Manhattan
3. A multi-family portfolio in Colorado
4. A large retail shopping center in California
5. A portfolio of CVS and Walgreens stores located in Southern states

How does a DST work? A trustee of the DST initially purchases the property and takes title. The Sponsor of the DST, the party who typically arranges the bank financing and coordinates the management of the property, then structures the transaction and arranges for sale of beneficial interests to individual investors. Though the beneficial interests are considered to be securities under federal securities laws, for purposes of 1031 Exchanges, Revenue Ruling 2004-86 states that a beneficial interest in a DST is considered "like-kind" real estate.

According to DST proponents, these are some of the benefits of DST ownership:

1. DSTs can offer higher quality, investment grade assets that are typically only available to large institutions
2. DSTs provide investors with current income
3. DST investors have no management or day-to-day operation responsibilities
4. The debt is non-recourse, which means that in the event of a default, the DST investor is not personally liable

Of course, DSTs are not suited for all. Investors who enjoy managing the day-to-day operations of their properties may not be good candidates. A DST is also not for an investor who wishes to invest in property for a short period since DST investments are typically designed for a holding period of an average of five to seven years. Additionally, DSTs are designed for "accredited investors" which are high net worth individuals as defined in Regulation D of the Securities Act of 1933.

Given the intricacies of purchasing suitable real estate assets and structuring these offerings, from both a securities and tax perspective, exchangers and their advisors should perform due diligence when selecting a DST Sponsor. The Sponsor will provide a Private Placement

Memorandum ("PPM") which provides information about the properties, area demographics, leases, projections and other important disclosures. Due diligence emphasis should be placed on real estate, property management and asset management expertise, prior performance track record, experience with sophisticated financing structures, transparent investor communications, financial strength of the Sponsor and excellent legal representation."

DSTs have risks like all real estate and carry fees and expenses which may offset some of the benefits of tax deferral.

Ok, so there you have a good look at what some serious independent research is stating and a pretty respectable disclosure also. I will tell you 80% of what I am seeing are multi-family residential DSTs 300 to 400 units. And if you get the chance you will likely be impressed at the high level of management and software sophistication used to keep these properties operational.

Their algorithms measure and track every bit of data both on site and off on a daily basis. And while we're at it, investors receive quarterly management and budget reports. It is a very transparent process.

Having worked with investment property owners for years, I have seen many transformations from active manager to passive investor. I have heard all the wonderful stories and new pursuits that come with freeing up more time and letting go of, at least for a few, some serious stress.

At some point owning investment properties can start to deplete your energy, or at the very least, interfere with fully immersing into retirement mode. For others, listing and selling properties and executing a 1031 Exchange into a DST investment grade property is simply a matter of taking advantage of a greatly appreciated property. Putting all that equity to work along with diversifying geographically and by asset class, often also potentially increases monthly income.

REAL ESTATE AGENTS:
THE BABY BOOMERS ARE COMING!

The leading edge of the baby boomers are, as of this writing, seventy-three years old. In many counties across the US, 30% of condos and residential property are owned as investment property, and in large part owned by this leading-edge baby boomer group.

The number one question I get from income property owners is, "Why doesn't my real estate agent know about this?" While real estate agents are in the business of buying and selling properties, DST investing is outside of their licensing and expertise.

More and more, investors expect real estate agents to collaborate and be familiar with strategies and solutions that are in the best interest of the client. So, my question to real estate agents is, "What are you saying to this huge group of investors and income property owners?" This is a formidable group of income property owners who want out of managing tenants and the headaches that come with it. This group of boomers is heading into full blown retirement mode.

So, at a time when listings are harder to come by, and the low hanging fruit for the most part is long gone, it is, as some real estate agents have discovered, wise to get into the planning mode and have a few strategies to put on the table.

Becoming a bit familiar with the DST as a 1031 Exchange can bring real solutions and create an abundance of listings.

ACTUAL STORIES

A real estate agent came to me who had nine properties. She had recently been diagnosed with a brain tumor on top of her many other health problems. She had concerns about leaving her husband with these properties; he had no experience in management, fixing things, or dealing with tenants.

"He's absolutely helpless," she said. She now has reduced her actively managed properties to four and has exchanged the other five for DSTs. She is so happy with the strategy she has often sent out blogs and e-mails to every real estate agent she knows, "I can't believe you are all not incorporating this DST strategy to create listings. There are so many investment property owners out there in my shoes."

Then there's Diane and her Mom. They had owned about a dozen units in a building for around thirty-five years. The property was aging, and it was two hours away, depending of course on traffic. Calls from tenants regarding problems in the building: plumbing, electrical, the usual stuff and occasionally not so usual, were becoming more frequent, making life more stressful. She and her mother had been at this for decades, but Diane had just remarried, and these issues revealed themselves as an early disruption in the marriage relationship.

When she heard about the DST solution, Diane jumped into immediate research mode and after two meetings and getting answers to two pages of questions, she was convinced that this was the best plan for her. Soon she had her property listed and sold her property for top dollar. She executed her first 1031 Exchange into three DST properties.

Three years later she smiles as she recalls the transactions. She said, "I'll never forget returning from a one-week cruise, coming into the kitchen to see my answering machine actually not even blinking.... No calls. Not even one. *Sigh.*"

Ted and Louise owned nineteen properties, for which Ted loved to be a hands-on manager. But he was getting up in years and starting to become forgetful. Louise is fifteen years younger, and she had long worried about what would happen when Ted leaves this world. She would be staring down the barrel of nineteen properties. She argued that Ted was obsessed with the properties, and that they owned him, rather than the other way around.

She went on to say that when you think about it, just to sell one property can be an ordeal. She would have to find a real estate agent, agree on listing parameters, show the property, accept an offer, go through the inspection process, respond to the list of inspection requests, and after all that, you often fall out of the first escrow. But by doing a 1031 Exchange into DST now before Ted passes on will save Louise the future stress of having to go through all those steps on her own.

Her having DST ownership gives her a transferable asset that requires no day-to-day management. And there will be no, as I like to call them, "accidental owners." That is, a beneficiary who does not have the desire or wherewithal to take on the management of the investment properties.

For many owners of investment properties, it is situations like these that prompt them to start thinking about an exit strategy. The DST 1031 Exchange is an effective way to do that while deferring taxes. And you can continue to do the 1031 Exchange forever. "Swap till you drop" is what they say in the industry. Not sure how that sounds, but there it is.

Many investment property owners are familiar with 1031 Exchanges. That's the term the industry uses when referring to Section 1031 of the U.S. Internal Revenue Service's tax code. The section provides that if an individual exchange one "like-kind" investment property for another, he or she may be able to defer capital gains or losses they otherwise would have to deal with at the time of an outright sale.

It is not unusual however to run into investors who have sold their properties, closed escrow without opening a 1031 escrow account that links to the traditional escrow. They call me after the fact and ask about the DST. At this point it is too late. You are on your way to a substantial tax event unless, of course, you have some loss to offset this transaction.

Many are stunned by the tax bill due in April. Some are prepared. Others try to make up for the lost income by investing in dividend stocks and bonds etc., only to find it will often take 10 years to break even from the tax loss, even if realizing a 5% return. The point here is, if you did a 1031 Exchange into a DST, you may even see your net monthly income increase, and not incur any tax liability.

Back to our previous example. For Louise, getting Ted to gradually exchange property for DSTs was like trying to pry his fingers, one by one, from a vice grip. Ted, like many investment property owners, was a control freak who wanted to be able to see, feel, and touch his property. Who can blame them? That's what has made them the successes that they are.

To keep peace in the household, Louise has been getting him to lighten the load gradually, and they are both very pleased with the results. And as it so often happens, once all that appreciated equity goes to work in a DST property, you'll more than likely be collecting more monthly income than with the property you were actively managing. Plus, DSTs have deferred capital gains and potentially increased depreciation benefits!

How Does a Delaware Statutory Trust (DST) Work?

A DST is a business trust created under Delaware law. It is a securitized investment that must comply with IRS Revenue Ruling 2004-86.

It allows investors to hold fractional shares in real estate properties – typically institutional grade. The properties are managed and administered by the Trustee for the financial benefit of the Trust beneficiaries (i.e. the investors who exchanged into the Delaware Statutory Trust). Investor options can be 100% cash (outright purchase of shares), but the most common method of investing is via a 1031 tax deferred Exchange.

DSTs offer investors property ownership benefits, just as if they were the sole owner of the property. With a DST ownership interest the investor typically receives monthly income, some of it sheltered by depreciation deductions and the like.

In the examples above, Diane and her Mom and Louise and Ted became the "beneficial owners" of a DST. They sold their properties through a traditional residential or commercial real estate broker, and stipulated in the sales contract that they were electing to do a tax deferred exchange with their proceeds.

Before they entered into a purchase and sale contract, they were working with me planning their exchange strategy into a DST. As an investment professional specializing in DSTs, I was and am in an ideal position to assist them as their investment representative. Real estate transactions are time sensitive. Have you ever heard the saying that "Time is of the essence?" That's the bell weather key to all real estate transactions. And I take it very seriously.

Part of my service is to follow the process closely. I prefer to start working for you at the outset until the goal is reached. Bring me on board immediately and I will be with you all along the way, looking after your interests making sure things get done right. My job begins the day you list your property, and finishes the day you have it sold and have exchanged into your new

DST investment. This complex process can be difficult to navigate and understand, something that I will help you with.

And to that end, I will make sure that critical time frames are adhered to, that you understand the process to your satisfaction, and that we find the most ideal DST to invest in, selecting the company and property type that works best for you.

My broad-based financial background may be of use in assisting in financial planning. Or it may be more focused on the transactional aspects of the DST exchange. Or it could be a combination of both. Whatever your needs may be, they will come to the fore front when we meet. It is important that we take the time to go over where you are and where you want to be. And then develop a strategy to that end. For instance, you may wish to exchange all of your equity into DST interests.

Or you may want to exchange part of your equity taking the balance in cash and paying tax on those proceeds. And you may elect to exchange part of your proceeds into a DST investment and the balance into another property that you would own outright while managing it yourself. There can be many factors contributing to the decision-making process and I look to explore those with you and help you identify what they are and how to deal with them.

My experience by the way, is that sometimes what seems to be obvious can easily be overlooked. Our meeting could prove to be critical in achieving optimum results for your future liquidity, current and future income as well and any life concerns that must all be considered. There is a whole discovery process which concludes with a determination of best fit for you, the investor.

One cannot predict what future health care issues or long-term care needs may surface. Concerns such as trust considerations, children, and any other issues need to be discussed.

To reiterate what was previously mentioned, there are very important time line rules that need to be adhered to. Having another set of eyes to watch out for your interests in that regard can be key. I will be in constant communication with the escrow officer with two key deadlines in mind: the 45 calendar days from the closing of the sale of the relinquished property that you have to identify the property(ies) you wish to trade into, and the 180 days from the closing of the sale you have to complete the acquisition of the new property.

Figure 1 is a visual of this process.

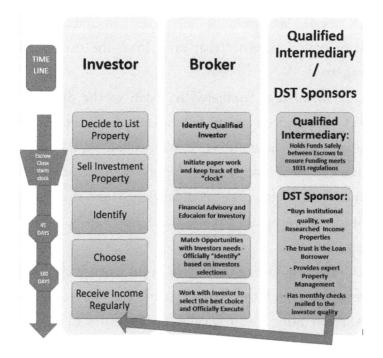

Figure 1: DST Basic Process Chart

Selecting potential DST investments is an interesting part of the process. The DST property may include multi-family units of two or three hundred units, or it could be healthcare-related office buildings, self-storage facilities, or triple net long term corporate leases like a Walgreens or a Napa Auto Parts or any number of companies. [In case the term is unfamiliar, a triple net lease is a **lease** in which the lessee pays rent to the lessor, as well as all taxes, insurance, and maintenance expenses that arise from the use of the property.]

I am always fascinated to listen to the Sponsor's DST acquisitions team talk about their acquisition criteria and how it is implemented. With more advanced technology and highly sophisticated and functional databases, competition for the most appropriate properties is keen and a proven Sponsor is important.

One thing I like to keep in mind when it comes to technology and the various market segments is the "Amazon Effect" as it is called. This relates to the fact that more consumers are purchasing items online and fewer are going to the "bricks and mortar" physical locations to purchase items. This has had a dramatic effect on the commercial real estate sector, especially retail.

However, some market segments seem immune to it, such as the housing market (people need a place to live) and the grocery store/convenience store market. Most investors, including the major DST Sponsors are aware of this and favor those sectors not so affected. As a DST advisor I stay on top of what property types are being offered and what the national real estate market trends are. Although difficult to predict, we still need to do the best we can to try to forecast what the future may hold relative to any particular real estate market segment.

Corporate entities that offer or sponsor DSTs are reviewed by me prior to my recommending any of their offerings. Part of my due diligence is to review information on the offering entities (Sponsors), making sure that their performance history, property selection process and quality of properties offered measures up to the high standards that I demand for my clients.

That criteria includes review of their financial disclosures, making sure that they are well-capitalized, review of their business credit rating which typically reflects their level of integrity, and performing telephone interviews with key personal confirming what the available data indicated.

At or about the time of placement (where one of my clients will be placing their funds into a DST share) I will have been carefully monitoring the equity available in the particular DSTs. Awareness as to the availability of a particular DST and the escrow target close dates are two of the most key components to ensure a successful completion of the 1031 DST exchange. Since I focus entirely on DSTs, and do so in a financial advisor capacity,

I can avoid common mistakes often made. For instance, every few months I walk into a situation where a well-meaning financial advisor will have stated to a client enthusiastically, "Sure I can do DSTs." They may be duly licensed to do so, but de facto unqualified! They don't realize the time commitment and responsibilities involved in helping an investor transition from an income property owner and manager to a DST investor!

On virtually every deal that I am involved with, I try to be as pro-active as possible doing what I can to make sure that no detail is overlooked, that nothing is missed, and that all of the moving parts work together smoothly and effectively to the successful completion of the transaction. It may seem unnecessary, but on the contrary, it often times proves to be key in getting the job done for the investors I work with.

Often that includes assuring the various parties that things are going as planned. That can include staying in touch with escrow officers (on the sale of the relinquished/traded property), the real estate agents involved, the investor and even the title company. On the DST side of things, gentle reminders and regular updates keeps them and their team at the ready. That includes the DST Sponsors themselves, their title company and the 1031 Exchanger handling the transfer of funds to close the deal. It can be pretty exciting watching all the pieces come together and making the call to the investor letting them know that they are now invested in a DST. It is one of my favorite calls to make!

A point that I would like to stress is that on the surface it may seem fairly straight forward, completing a 1031 Exchange into a DST interest, but it really is not. For instance, occasionally I get a call from someone working with another financial advisor trying to put a DST exchange together and they will tell me that it didn't go so well. Problems may have come up that were not properly addressed in advance.

The DST targeted may have sold out. There may have been a delay in the closing of the relinquished property and the available options changed. The investor/seller at the last minute may have chosen a different allocation of proceeds, affecting the planned DST exchange to where it was no longer doable. Those kinds of things can happen, and even more. It is so important to be working with someone who's primary business focus is helping investors invest in Delaware Statutory Trusts.

When you do this full time like I do, then the things required to provide the best service to your clients are the things that you do every day. Which is exactly what I love to do. Be sure that you find a specialist to work with in this field. We are living in the age of specialization and working with a specialist is always the best way to go.

THE STRENGTH OF A DST
SOLUTION

In the eyes of the IRS, a beneficial interest in a DST is considered a direct interest in real estate. The owner of that interest has the right to receive distributions from rental income or the sale of the property. At the same time the owner of that beneficial interest is not required to, and in most cases, does not have the responsibilities of managing the day to day operation of the property.

They are not required to manage the property to enjoy the full benefits of property ownership. The owner-investor has a purely passive relationship to the Trust's properties.

The title of the property is held by the Trust and not by the individual investors hence there is no liability to the individual on anything related to the property.

This includes any judgments or liens (typically quite rare in occurrence) or any financing placed on the property (quite common). Any loan on the property is considered non-recourse to the owner/investor.

This is in contrast to TIC (Tenant-In-Common) structures which were most popular in the 1990s and in the early 2000s. With TIC's individual investors were liable – the financing was "recourse." The non-recourse nature of the DST financing is one of a number of reasons why DSTs continue to gain in popularity with investors.

Because the DST is classified as a non-taxable entity, all profits (and losses) and accompanying tax liabilities are passed through to the investor. Nothing is guaranteed – but as a rule most DSTs will show a profit with some of that profit offset by allowable deductions.

Each DST is poised to place a large of amount of investor capital into acquiring the right property or portfolio of properties. They tend to operate at price point levels that few investors can. And for this reason, DSTs often times offer investors a chance to place equity into the kind of large-scale, high quality portfolios that are typically available only to institutional investors.

DSTs can, and often do, compete with institutional investors in acquiring real estate, which represents another factor in risk mitigation. Most institutions are highly risk averse when they invest in anything, with real estate no exception.

In terms of financing the property, primarily financing as part of the acquisition process, the Sponsors of the DST will arrange it on behalf of the DST. Investors are not involved in the financing process and therefore have no responsibility or duties in that regard. The signatory trustee of the DST remains in that capacity for the duration of the DST ensuring continuity of management and oversight of DST activities, property ownership and management.

Mark Kosanke, former PricewaterhouseCooper Senior Corporate Auditor/CPA, 14 years ADISA board member and former president writes the following, which underscores how the DST guidelines protect the investors with the limits imposed on the Trustee.

LIMITS ON THE POWER OF A DST TRUSTEE

They're known as the "Seven Deadly Sins." They are limits set on the power of a DST trustee by IRS ruling 2004-86.

We mentioned the IRS ruling 2004-86; so, what's that all about? OK, —Here it is:

1) **Once the offering is closed, there can be no future capital contributions to the DST** by either current or new beneficiaries. To allow further contributions would dilute the original investors' percentages of ownership.

2) **The trustee cannot renegotiate the terms of any existing mortgage loans, nor can it obtain any new mortgage financing from any party except when a property tenant is bankrupt or insolvent.** If a trustee were allowed to assume greater liabilities (and thus increase risk), it would be doing so without the consent, and possibly to the dissatisfaction, of the beneficiaries.

3) **The trustee cannot enter into new leases or renegotiate existing leases except when a property tenant is bankrupt or insolvent.** DSTs operate best when their invested properties are under long-term leases to credit-worthy tenants. These types of leases mean the investment may offer greater protection.

4) **The trustee cannot reinvest the proceeds from the sale of its real estate.** The IRS

ruling requires that all proceeds from a DST investment should be distributed to investors. It is they who have the right to determine how to reinvest the capital.

5) **The trustee is limited to making the following types of capital expenditures with respect to the property: (a) expenditures for normal repair and maintenance of the property; (b) expenditures for minor non-structural capital improvements of the property, and (c) expenditures for repairs or improvements required by law.** The trustee cannot make a major upgrade to the property, such as adding new units to a complex or building a clubhouse; there is no assurance that costs for this would be recouped at the time of sale. Less major value-added upgrades like upgrading apartment interiors or adding a dog park or a fitness center are permissible.

6) **All cash, other than necessary reserves, must be distributed to the investors on a current basis.** DST trustees are allowed to keep a reserve of cash for repairs or other unexpected expenses. They are required, however, to make distributions to

beneficiaries within the expected time frame.

7) **Any cash held between distribution dates can only be invested in short-term debt obligations.** A short-term debt is considered the equivalent of cash because it can be readily re-converted to cash for distribution to investors. So now that I've listed all these, I'll tell you the Sponsors that offer the DST property are, as you can well imagine, all over these points.

Governed of course by Delaware State Law, if a DST Trustee/Sponsor that violates any of these restrictions the DST is allowed to convert into a Limited Liability Company (LLC).

The consequences of the "springing LLC" is primarily that the investor cannot 1031 exchange out of the LLC. This is a safety net to protect investors as the investors would then have voting rights relative to the decisions made in the operation and management of the property. This includes the decision to sell the property. At the same time, they remain free from any liabilities associated with ownership that extend beyond the amount that they have already invested.

HERE ARE SOME THINGS TO KEEP IN MIND ABOUT DST THAT ARE OFTEN IN THE DISCLOSURES PROVIDED:

A DST is a securities product with real estate at its core. These are some of the factors a would-be investor should consider:

- DSTs may not be suitable for investors who want to continue managing their properties.
- DSTs may not be suitable for those seeking only a short-term investment. DSTs are typically designed for a holding period of 5-7 years and can be up to 10 years.
- DSTs have risks like all real estate, are illiquid, and have fees and expenses associated with the purchase, which may reduce the bottom-line dollar amount goes directly into acquiring an asset. These fees and expenses can also offset some or all of the benefits of the tax deferral.
- DSTs are designed for "accredited investors," individuals of high net worth or income level, as defined by Regulation D of the Securities Act of 1933. At the time of this writing, this equates to a net worth of over one million dollars, but not including principal residence, or an annual income

of $200,000 (or $300,000 combined with spouse) for the last two years and expected in the next.

- Because of the complexities of selecting and structuring real estate offerings, would-be investors and their registered representative need to exercise due diligence in choosing a DST Sponsor. The Sponsor will provide a Private Placement Memorandum (PPM). This provides information about the properties, such as area demographics, leases, and projections.

- The investor and the registered representative should consider a Sponsor's expertise at property and asset management, the Sponsor's track record, the Sponsor's experience with sophisticated financing structures, its financial strength and legal representation, and the transparency of its communication with investors.

- The investor should remember that real estate is subject to the cycles of the economy, just like other investments. The value of a property may drop because of factors such as variations in occupancy, oversupply of space in an area, increases in operating costs, tenant defaults, a change in interest rates, adverse changes in laws, etc.

- There is no guarantee that investment objectives will be achieved.

Untapped Wealth for Philanthropy

Regardless of how an investor chooses to dispose of their real estate (sale, inheritance or gift) the issue of a potential capital gains tax should be a primary concern. The risks investors have taken and the "sweat equity" they have put into their real estate investments normally make them very adverse to seeing 20-50% of their real estate equity evaporate because of the capital gains tax.

It is very important to realize that paying the capital gains tax not only costs the investor the *present value* of their money but also the *future value* as well. This is also important to note as an investor in their mid-60's can expect to live into their mid-80's. Those tax dollars, if kept re-invested instead, could double or triple over that 20-year period of time. This future value is lost if the investor sells their real estate outright and simply pays the taxes. Rarely ever a good idea.

The ability to defer the taxes on the sale of real estate has been the primary driver for executing 1031 Tax Deferred Exchanges. The unique benefits of a DST are accelerating that demand.

> "The industry has come a long way in the past 15 years, what used to be triple net properties and credit leases now is anchored in multi-family properties. What used to be a cottage industry is now a multi-billion-dollar industry and growing fast. We're now seeing some alternative strategies in self-storage, health care, student housing and industrial.
>
> This diversification is bringing in new investors. Now two decades of legacy is certainly demonstrating the viability of full cycle programs that this does work. It is no longer a cottage industry. A constant re-tooling of expenses and costs really is quite a vindication of the industry moving forward."
>
> Per Keith Lampi, President of Inland Private Capital Corporation –
> January 2020, DIWIRE e-publication.

To re-emphasize, some of the unique benefits DSTs provide are:

1. Access to institutional quality real estate
2. Elimination of all landlord responsibilities. It is a 100% passive investment.
3. Elimination of *recourse* debt on the relinquished real estate. The comparable financing on the DST is *nonrecourse.*
4. Creation of potential monthly income.
5. Ability to provide diversification. The minimum DST investment is $100K. There is no maximum investment. This allows the investor to diversify their real estate assets by investing in multiple DSTs or investing in DSTs with multiple properties within the DST structure. The amount of transactions in the upper end is growing noticeably in the last few years.

SO, WHAT DOES THIS HAVE TO DO WITH PHILANTHROPY? QUITE A BIT!

As an income property owner, the investor may not be able to donate their property to the charity of their choice as that charity may not be able to accept real estate as a donation.

However, investing in a DST may essentially accomplish the same thing. So, let's look at this in terms of the benefits and opportunities DSTs can create as a philanthropic tool.

First: Virtually every investor is constantly being asked to give to some charity, non-profit, school, hospital or cause. The requests for contributions are unceasing and reach a fevered pitch as the calendar year ends. Year-end requests are trying to capture a last-minute tax deduction on the part of the donor.

The pressure for most non-profits as the year comes to an end is relentless. In fact, many non-profits depend on year end giving to make or break their budgets. The donation of a portion or all of the income generated by a DST ownership interest would create both predictability and stability to the beneficiary.

DST income is typically generated on a monthly basis over a five to seven-year time frame [best guess.] For the charity receiving such a gift there is no need to incur the cost of another capital campaign, golf tournament, direct mail campaign or any of the other fund-raising strategies currently being used to maintain that income stream.

Second: Most if not all non-profits are soliciting donors without consideration being given to ideas that might be value added to the donor. If fund raising efforts would incorporate ideas and strategies that would benefit potential donors at the outset those charities may find that their donations increase. Making the effort to genuinely help the donor before asking the donor to help the non-profit can create a symbiotic mutually beneficial relationship meeting the needs of both.

For instance, presenting an idea to a donor, who owns highly appreciated real estate, that solves the donor's real estate tax issues could be a great starting point. And with this kind of insight and expertise available it may be much easier for a donor to decide to donate a portion of the their recently acquired DST income as a way to help a non-profit. Offering a clear path to donations that makes sense to donors is an example of the adage "Give something of value before asking for something in return."

Third: Owners/Investors want control, so do most non-profit beneficiaries! As people age, a couple of emotions begin to play a bigger role in their lives. One is control. There are people who do not donate anything who would do so, and perhaps quite a bit, if their giving did not mean giving up control of their assets.

Moreover, as a practical matter, most non-profits want to control/own the asset and not just the income it produces. They want to own the "goose" and not just the "eggs." It may well be that a better strategy for potential beneficiaries (in order to generate more donors and more income) would be to focus primarily on the income and leave control of the asset with the donor. This way the donor maintains "control" and yet is committed to the donation. This strategy also de facto may create an endowment like structure where the income stream remains over time as the value of the dedicated asset increases.

Another common feeling for older people often times is fear: Fear of losing their money, fear of losing their social position, fear of outliving their money, fear of the future. Encouraging investors to maintain control of their assets by essentially maintaining the status quo (with the benefits and convenience of a DST investment) is a way to offset some of those fears, yet still empower them to donate!

Fourth: Most non-profits do not want and or cannot accept donations of real estate. In most cases, donated real estate becomes more of a burden than a blessing. The non-profit typically does not have the staff or the technical ability to manage real estate or even the wherewithal to outsource that function. Donated properties may be located out of state, may have unknown/undisclosed but significant issues such as environmental, municipal code or zoning violations, construction defects, clouds on title (claims of others attached to the property) and the like.

The non-profit will most likely sell the real estate as soon as possible in order to mitigate any risks associated with property ownership. To facilitate a quick sale all too often the property is offered at a discount relative to the fair market value, which means that the non-profit is not receiving the full benefit of the donation. However, because of the benefits to the investor and the potential beneficiary, another option in achieving the goal of donating their property would be to execute a 1031 tax deferred Exchange into a DST ownership interest.

At that point, if the donor wants, they can donate their interest in the DST (which is a fair market value interest). And furthermore, they are now donating an interest in an institutional quality asset. In this case the non-profit gets both the goose and the egg.

Fifth: This has to do with the number of different trust strategies available as estate planning tools. The fact is that there is no "one size fits all" when it comes to trust and estate planning. One trust option as a donation vehicle is the Charitable Remainder Trust (CRT). A significant factor to consider relative to a CRT is that real estate with any debt on it (a leveraged property) cannot be put into a CRT.

When real estate properties have debt on them (financed properties) the DST is perhaps a more appropriate substitute a to the CRT. A CRT simply will not qualify. And even if the property qualifies for a CRT, consideration should be given to the costs associated with establishing a trust. Real estate investors with assets valued in the lower range may find that the costs relative the value of the asset being placed in a CRT are enough to make the CRT option not feasible.

For example, if the property has a taxable long-term capital gain of $100-$200K it probably does not make economic sense to establish and maintain a CRT or some other trust structure. However, since the minimum for a DST investment is only $100K it makes it certainly possible for the investor to address his tax and/or charitable goals without incurring the relatively high cost of setting up and maintaining a separate trust.

Sixth: In a very unique way, the 1031/DST-charity strategy combines both tax deferral with tax deduction which makes it a win-win—a win for the donor, a win for the charity.

Knowing your options can save some hand wringing and sleepless nights, wondering why you either didn't know about the DST or knew about them but did not choose them as the alternative to solving your real estate needs. As a matter of fact, recently two investors each owning income property in the $20 million range came to me: one wanted to try and figure out how they could get out of their CRT, and the other their UPREIT.

A little buyer's remorse perhaps? With a DST on average every 5-7 years (this is just an average—not a guarantee) you can reset your position as the DST properties are sold. The DST offers potential for long term investment flexibility. The CRT does not. At the time the DST liquidates the assets you have the option to roll over to another DST, exchange into another property that you wish to buy on your own account, make a partial exchange and take out some of your equity realizing a capital gain on that amount or simply liquidate and pay the tax on the entire gain. When the DST sells its properties, you can elect to reinvest or make a new decision. A 1031/DST strategy for philanthropic purposes is a new and different approach from what has been historically implemented when it comes to real estate and fund raising.

What makes this strategy so potentially effective – better than the previously dominant ones is the timing. The baby boomer age wave that has driven our economic trends since the 1950's is coming full circle. Aging baby boomers are looking to dispose of their real estate holdings.

At the same time, the aging process is causing people to think about legacy, giving back, and in particular to their college, local hospital, favorite ministry or charity. What 1031s and DSTs bring to the world of philanthropy is a tool for benefitting both the donor and the charity. Because there is so much wealth embedded in highly appreciated real estate, the opportunity to find a better way to access that wealth for the benefit of philanthropy could not be greater. It will be to the advantage of every professional engaged in any way with real estate, tax planning, estate planning or philanthropy to become fully knowledgeable about DSTs and the benefits they could bring to the table as replacement real estate in a 1031 Like Kind Exchange.

The DST is poised to get more momentum and gain traction with regard to charitable giving. The concept will surely become an avenue for larger institutions to harness otherwise inaccessible funds. The DST could also be a bridge for donors that are reluctant to give too much too soon.

GETTING STARTED

To invest in a DST, you need to work with a qualified registered DST representative. Whether you want to purchase an interest with cash or exchange equity in an investment property for a DST interest, finding the right representative to assist you is key. In the latter case – exchanging – the process is complex and needs to be managed carefully.

The transition of selling your property, putting the proceeds into a 1031 escrow account, identifying the right DST Sponsor and property, and finally placing your funds into the DST completing the process may seem to be an overwhelming undertaking. And this is what I help you with, assisting in every step of the way making sure that deadlines are met, the paper work is in order and things happen when and how they are supposed to. As in most professions, there are a core of individuals who are positioned to provide this service. But of that group there are very few that specialize specifically on DST investments. I am one of those. In my 20 years of experience, I have learned to stick to the fundamentals with effective communication being the primary. I find that I am virtually in constant communication with the internal staffs at these various DST real estate Sponsors.

Things can change and by staying in touch I can keep abreast of those changes passing along key information and insights to the people that I represent. On an almost daily basis I am briefed on availability in terms of dollars that can be placed into their various DST offerings. It is not unusual for investors to have quite intricate questions of me about various aspects of the program. I am able to field those questions and get the answers due to my ready access to the Sponsors staff and support personnel.

We want to educate the investor and more importantly, make sure that the DST option is a good fit. A big part of that is to explain DST rules and how the investment will work. Some investors tend to do their own research and educate themselves. Just the same, I always make a point of going over the basics no matter how well learned someone may be. My many years of transactional experience provides me with insight that can only be gained with time. I have seen the twists and turns that can occur and I am here to assist you navigate the course.

You may be someone who has owned the same property for 30, 40, or even 50 years. And quite naturally you may feel like you know your property inside and out: every electrical outlet, plumbing fixture, roofing improvement, sidewalk, garage, every last detail. Don't feel like you are alone, as many of the investors that I have and are working with are in a similar situation.

For them I have found that often times it is difficult for them to contemplate having someone else manage it, much less selling the property! And–yet, when that day comes and I am fortunate enough to assist, the end result often times is that they have transitioned from owning as an individual – with all of the demands that entails – to owning as an investor in a trust; with virtually no demands yet all of the benefits.

There are some investors that I work with that are very pragmatic and see their property as stock in trade. It's a business asset and making the decision to trade into a DST is as much numbers driven as life style driven.

Those people tend to minimize any emotional attachment to their property making the decision process somewhat easier for them. To those, the math simply works out. The numbers line up, their equity goes to work in a DST, monthly income continues, the tax write-offs are there, and the depreciation clock is reset.

It's a simple concept that deserves to be emphasized: With a DST investment, the burden of management and maintenance, is long gone by trading the investor's well-earned equity into DST equity shares in institutional grade properties.

DO NO HARM: HEALTHY INVESTMENT STRATEGY MY PLEDGE TO YOU

My number one rule in advising clients is fashioned from what they teach at Harvard Medical School: Do no harm.

As an investment professional, I am a specialist with a focus on the 1031 Exchange area of real estate as it relates to DST income real-estate. I am considered by others to be a pioneer in the industry, as early on I saw the tremendous benefits and the need for placing investors into DST via the 1031 Exchange route. And at the time based on what I was hearing from the Sponsors I was working with – I was one of the first to see it and act on it. Over time my instincts have proven spot on. DSTs work and they work well.

That being said, I have an obligation to my clients to consider their entire portfolio of investments and I take that obligation seriously. Having worked as a money manager I am familiar with the myriad of options available to investors. And if it appears as though DSTs may not be in their best interest, I will tell them so.

I recently advised an investor after a lengthy meeting to consider an Airbnb for one of his properties. For him, his life circumstances and the location of his properties all wrapped together; that was a good option I thought he should have on the table. In this particular case, the investor was 52 years old, and he had a successful restaurant that was on auto pilot. He had nothing but time on his hands during the week and seemed to be looking for a project at this time in his life.

I introduced him to a friend of mine who shared her recent experiences with the Airbnb model. A year later he is still perfecting his Airbnb property, but he also decided to do a 1031 Exchange into a DST with one of his other properties. That particular property was not giving him the kind of return that the DST option provided.

Another benefit to investing in DSTs is that you have the option to diversify. Low minimums and relatively painless closing process makes it easy to diversify in several different DSTs. It is not necessary to place 100% of your exchange funds into just 1 DST. You have options. And those options are not only property type (apartments, shopping centers office buildings, etc.) but also location. DSTs invest in properties all over the country – not just in the state where you live! In my opinion in order to reduce risk, it is wise to diversify. The best bet is to have a mix, a variety of holdings.

Let's turn now to what is, perhaps, the prime motivator of 1031 Exchanges and DSTs: deferring capital gains taxes. In a conversation with Geoff Flahardy, another one of the pioneers of the industry and one of my favorite go-to guys, he provided the following information.

> "First, let's be sure about what capital gains are. Say you purchased a property a few years ago, and then made a lot of improvements to it. When you sell, the capital gain is the

difference between the sales price minus the closing costs on the one hand, and what you paid for the property plus what you put into it on the other. The price you paid plus the cost of improvements is known as your cost basis.

If you have taken a loan on your property, that must be paid off at the time of sale, but it doesn't reduce your capital gain. The amount of this debt, however, as well as the equity you've received, can be transferred into a DST. The rules make the math work out that way."

In fact, under the rules for 1031 Exchanges, the new investment and any debt on the properties must be equal to or greater than the old. This is the government's way of encouraging new investments to stimulate the economy. Most DSTs come packaged with a new loan, usually about 45% to 65% loan to value as it's called. The individual investor does not have to go through a loan process. The DST Sponsor does that; the loan is secured by the property and is non-recourse to the investor.

There are a number of potential advantages to increasing equity and debt in a DST. The investment is larger and thus the possibility of growth in equity is larger. Value is also increased through debt with a higher loan-to-value. The investor is not responsible if the loan should default. It should be noted that higher debt can also increase the risk in a property. Let's take a closer look at the new debt and the new possible depreciation schedule, and what it will mean.

Here's an example, prepared for us by Geoff Flarhardy, the national accounts director of ExchangeRight of Pasadena, California:

> Relinquished Property Value: $1,000,000
> Replacement Property Purchase Value: $2,000,000
> Loan-to-Value: 50%
> Surplus value acquired: $1,000,000
> Land Value: 20% = $200,000 (You cannot depreciate land value.)
> Improvement Value = $800,000
> Asset Class: Commercial – 39-year depreciation schedule
> Cost recovery = $20,512.82 ($800,000/39)
> If the DST is paying 6%, then $20,512,82 of the $60,000 of income would be sheltered, or 34.19%.
> **NOTE:** This is just an example and should not be considered a model for tax purposes.

*Basis is the term for the cost of a property for tax purposes. It begins with the purchase price of the property and is increased as improvements are made but decreased for items such as depreciation. The difference between the sales price of the property and the adjusted basis will result in the figure for capital gains that are taxable.

HOW IT ALL STARTED FOR ME

I have been a registered representative since 1990 and spent most of those years as a portfolio manager. I soon realized that real estate and related investments were really my passion. So, when a CPA, formerly of Pricewaterhouse, let me know that there were new regulations in place that would allow for real estate investors to sell their properties and complete 1031 tax deferred exchanges into interests in DSTs, I was pretty excited. It caught my attention and I wanted to get involved.

People who owned, rehabbed and managed their properties always impressed me. For me, that seemed to be much more rewarding than engaging in and experimenting with stock strategies. Chasing short term gains in the stock market only to find that most of the trades don't pan out as planned never really appealed to me.

It has been much more rewarding utilizing 1031 Exchange strategies to help investors find exit strategies that will free up their time and help get them into retirement mode in which they can better enjoy the fruits of their labors.

Most investors are savvy when it comes to managing their real estate and their money. They can do the math and they have great intuition. My role is to put the facts on the table for them, and to answer their questions in what usually turns out to be a lengthy but satisfying due diligence process.

Typically, I want to hear your story, what you have to say. Which means that in our first meeting you will find that I do a lot of listening. People that I help can be in various stages of the process. Some are planning an exit strategy for two or three years in the future. Others have already listed their properties and started work on a 1031 Exchange.

Regardless of where they are, my role is to listen, and to listen carefully. Why are they selling? Is it because of stress? Is income replacement a key issue? They may own several properties. They may just recently have heard about DSTs. Are they familiar with 1031 Exchanges? I am!

I may need to explain what the 1031 Exchange process entails, from closing the sale of the property they currently own, why and how their sale proceeds are sent to and held by a third party "accommodator," and finally when their funds will be wired to the DST property, representing the completion of the process.

THE FOUNDATION, TRUST AND INTEGRITY OF THIS INDUSTRY STARTED WITH INLAND

In my opinion the industry exists and has such a high standard of operation because of one great American company by the name of Inland Group of Real Estate Companies. It is the grandfather of the industry. Inland set the bar so high to begin with, their ethics and integrity are for all to follow.

When talking about DSTs, the names of a few other real estate companies must be talked about in some detail. But I am going to focus mainly on The Inland Group of Real Estate Companies. And yes, there are others like ExchangeRight, and newcomer to the DST industry, the 80-year-old New York Bond company

Cantor Fitzgerald. You may remember them from 9/11 as they lost many employees in the World Trade Center collapse. There are several others I could add to the list, but I have to start with what can only be called a great American story: the heralded and greatly admired for their ethics and investor-first reputation. I'd like you to meet Inland.

THE INLAND REAL ESTATE COMPANIES

If there is a 600-pound gorilla in the DST industry, it is the Inland Group of Real Estate Companies. They have been around for 50 years. Inland's motto is "Good Deeds. Since 1968." The name Inland also is not only a play on words— "In Land," but it was chosen to reflect the idea that the whole company is more than the sum of its parts.

It was started by a group of school teachers, if you can imagine that. Now Inland stands out as the industry leader in creating, developing, and supporting real estate investment funds. Inland companies have sponsored more than 700 investment programs for about half a million investors. Inland controls about 40 percent of the market. Everything about Inland, its acquisition process, management style, and investor services, all of it is held to the highest ethical standard.

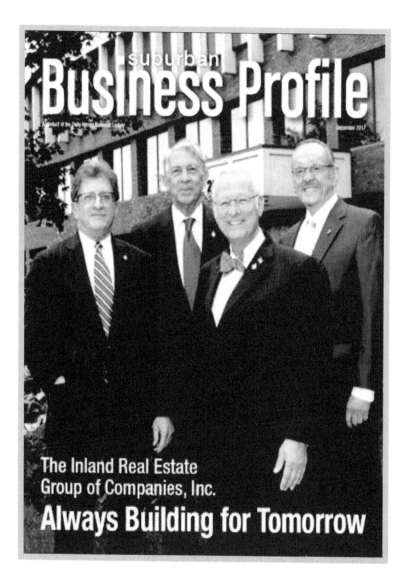

suburban
Business Profile

The Inland Real Estate
Group of Companies, Inc.
Always Building for Tomorrow

And that's what you might expect from a company
that was founded by four Chicago public school

teachers. The first people to invest in the company founded by Dan Goodwin, Bob Baum, Joe Cosenza and Bob Parks were also school teachers, or their own families and friends. Their founding notion was that real estate was a basic human need, and therefore a reliable investment stream.

Their motivation for starting Inland was the need to increase their income above the $6,000/year salary they got as teachers. They began by pooling their money, $100 here, $500 there, then building houses and small apartment buildings and opening a real estate brokerage business. They did all of the work themselves: painting, decorating, and selling the properties. That took a lot of time, but in the early years they had it. They were free each day after 3:15 p.m., and then of course, there were weekends. They were very successful. Very successful. Within five years, all four of them quit their teaching jobs to devote their full time to Inland.

About 10 years after its founding, Inland had acquired over 10,000 apartment units which they were managing for the company's limited partners. Each complex was a different partnership. Joe Cosenza, now with the title of Vice Chairman of The Inland Real Estate Group, LLC and President of Inland Real Estate Acquisitions, says that at the time the properties were regional -he was able to drive to all of them. All being located in the Midwest, Illinois, Wisconsin, and northern Indiana and not that very far from Chicago made that feasible. At that time Inland also owned related businesses, like construction, waste removal and pest control.

By 1981, Inland reached a milestone, having placed over $100 million of investor funds into limited partnerships. By 1985, the company and its investors owned approximately 42,000 apartments all managed by Inland. That year, according to Cosenza: "We did one other thing that was new. And that was, we formed the first *public* limited partnership. All the rest of them had to have, like, 35 investors. You could expand that a little bit but that's all you could have. That's what the rules were, what the SEC rules were.

So, we decided, why don't we, even though no one knows us around the country, why don't we do public limited partnerships so we could sell in every state and buy in every state then too. We did. It was very smart because we started to do it, and we did it without any more hitches on any of the properties."

But a big hitch in Inland's businesses came in 1986. That's when the Tax Reform Act removed many benefits from real estate investments, even retroactively.

Cosenza calls it a "disaster" that sent real estate prices plummeting and literally crushed all savings-and-loans over the next few years. Without S&Ls, real estate companies had a tough time financing investments.

Developers couldn't finance improvements, and jobs were lost all across the board, from legal and financial services to the people who did construction, painting, carpeting and so forth.

Inland's response to this crisis is admirable and noteworthy. Cosenza again: "Toward the end of the '80s, 1988, '89, we did a couple of things. One, we had about 400 limited partnerships by then, but the bottom 10% weren't worth what they were when the investors went into them. So, the four of us took almost the whole year to figure out how we could save these people, because we couldn't live with anybody losing money with us.

And so, we came up with a couple of ideas. The first idea was, if we could get with a public company and do a sale-leaseback to them on their real estate, and they were a healthy company, we could buy that. We could have the investors vote to sell the one that wasn't so good, and whatever money they had they could put into the new one, and we would put in the rest of the money out of our pockets."

That's how Inland became the landlord for Wal-Mart, in fact Wal-Mart's biggest landlord for the next 20 years. Cosenza says the deal cost the four partners $17 million, but "nobody lost money with us at the time, and we all (could) sleep well."

In the 1990s, Inland focused more on commercial properties like shopping centers, industrial properties, and vacant land suitable for development. In 1994, Inland formed its first Real Estate Investment Trust, or REIT (pronounced "Reet"). REITs became popular because they could be publicly sold on the New York Stock Exchange. They are modeled after mutual funds and each REIT can have thousands of investors.

Inland's first REIT contained 140 shopping centers. Inland decided to go into retail because the retail industry was on the upswing after a slump in the late 1980s. The second REIT came in 2000 and focused on properties in the South and all along the East Coast. The third REIT included properties in the West. In total, Inland has formed eight REITS with assets in the tens of billions of dollars.

When Inland began, its partnerships were formed as Illinois Land Trusts. That's all that was available. There could be multiple investors in a trust, and their identities were protected. Each investor could sell his/her share, and the lender holding the paper on the trust needn't give approval. The lenders liked the trusts because the trust was the title-holder and the signer of the mortgage. In the 1990s, Cosenza became aware of something called the Delaware Business Trust. It was similar to an Illinois Land Trust, but it was available in all of the states. Inland got its team of lawyers to work on ways to structure a Delaware Business Trust like an Illinois Land Trust.

After thousands and thousands of dollars of legal fees, sure enough, we could structure it to have multiple owners, and most importantly, you could structure it so that if an individual is inside this trust, he can sell his partnership interest in exchange for someone's fee (ownership) interest in another property. Or vice versa. In other words, if someone sells their fee interest (ownership) in a property; up to that time the IRS guidelines would only allow fee simple interest in one property to be traded for a fee simple interest in another property.

But the rules were modified to allow for the exchange of a fee simple interest in one property for a partnership interest in a trust that owns another property. The investor does not have to specifically be the owner of record on the new property as before. This was the key change in the regulations that helped spawn the DST revolution. We were given the ability to make a land trust and the beneficial interest in that land trust would be treated just like a direct ownership interest, so that the person who sold his property could complete a "like kind" 1031 tax exchange into a beneficial interest of a DST trust. And Voila! The Delaware Statutory Trust was born. Actually, in the year 2000, the state of Delaware made the name change from Business Trust to Statutory Trust. You could call Joe Cosenza the "Father of the DST" but he is more modest, crediting Inland, the corporation, as the father. He does say however, that Inland was, without a doubt, one of the forerunners in the industry.

In 2001, Inland formed its Private Capital Corporation for 1031 Exchange investors. It now has six billion dollars in assets. It has raised three billion from people who decided to sell their properties and trade into one of the many offerings brought to the market by Inland. Cosenza explains:

"Now each Delaware Statutory Trust owns one building. Maybe it owns two buildings. But they're all separate on their own. And stand on their own. And in the course of the years… one of the things we did different than any other company was that we bought the assets first, we financed it first, inside that Delaware

Statutory Trust so that when an investor saw the deal, it was already clean. It was already completed, and now they could exchange into it, without any worry that the deal may have fallen through, or that the loan was different from what they thought they saw on paper. We would never do that. Other companies did, and they caused disasters in the marketplace."

Long term success and market dominance is a testament to the fact that Inland has strict standards for its DST business and the properties it acquires and faithfully adheres to them: "it's got to be, of course, scrutinized left and right by Inland with due diligence, got to pass our due diligence standards, got to pass the standards of enough of a cash flow. It's got to pass the standards of a lender to lend against it. Usually we do 55% financing. Safe.

"When you're around the 50% level there's a lot of room there before you will ever get hurt. And then lastly, the due diligence is performed by broker dealers, financial planners, who sell this. Now keep in mind, we've dealt with financial planners since the 1970s, some of which we're still dealing with. Anyhow, when you deal in that world, now you're dealing with securities. So now you have another threshold of due diligence. The broker-dealers do their due diligence with the financial planners, and you have to pay them for the cost of their due diligence. So, if they pass it, now you've got two complete sets of due diligence done. On the real estate level, the securities level, and the real estate level again… That's why we have 40 percent of the business across the country…We have very high standards."

It is not always a person who is selling or has sold a property who wants to invest in a DST. About 30 percent of investors want to invest because of the return on the investment in terms cash flow. They also may find appealing a property being offered in a DST. Cosenza says he does that himself.

Lenders like DSTs for several reasons: a DST is a single entity, not the 100 or 200 or more people who are invested. They tend to invest in high quality real estate. They take conservative positions in terms of loan to value ratios (55% as typical as noted above). The properties almost always are professionally managed and they tend to have only one or two points of contact for the lender to deal with, making it that much easier to do business with them.

All of these factors combined mitigate the risk factor from the lenders point of view, reducing the probability of foreclosing for non-performance and/or bankruptcy. The life of each DSTs varies. The time from inception to dissolution of the property(ies) may go out as long as 10 years, with a 5 to 7 average full cycle duration. The length is determined by the initial plan for the holdings and also the marketplace.

Changes may occur during ownership prompting an earlier than planned dissolution or a delay in the dissolution. In any event it is the Sponsor, like Inland, who determines when its time sell with an eye focused on the best results for the investor partners.

As for the costs to investors, Cosenza explains: "All the fees are exposed. They have to be. First of all, you've got a broker-dealer who gets a fee, it's usually about six percent, and then you have to pay for their due diligence. They've got to do real estate and securities and that's about one and a quarter percent. And then you have ours which is about two to two and a half percent. And anything else, third party reports. You have to have an engineering report. You've got to know that bricks-and-mortar isn't sinking. You've got to know it's got no mold. You've got to know all this stuff because you might not be able to see it visually. Then you have to have an environmental report. You don't know what's in that ground.... Appraisal and lender fees. The lender might charge you half a point. All those fees are right there, upfront."

When the housing bubble burst in 2008 Inland felt the pain. But it also saw the opportunity. Real estate prices dropped, and Inland responded!

As for the future, Cosenza doesn't foresee much change in the DST market unless Congress again acts to change the tax laws like it did in 1986. Cosenza points all the way back to 1921. That's when Congress first enacted like-kind exchange rules. The idea was to allow investors to trade up and those with lower income to get into the investment market in the first place. The intent was to encourage investment and grow the economy. It worked.

In the commercial real estate retail segment, there's a market trend often referred to as "The Amazon Effect." Cosenza says "Amazon is a killer. They're murderers. They're slayers." He's talking about the negative consequences to retailers who are losing business to Amazon. But he says Amazon can't do everything. Inland is interested in places where people may go two or three times a week, like grocery stores. Or other businesses Amazon can't replace: like gas stations, cleaners, the local ice cream store, or the corner liquor store.

That's why they invest in and those types of centers are all over the country. Cosenza and Inland are very proud of the commitment the company has made to the communities in which it operates. In 2009, the Better Business Bureau gave Inland its first Torch Award for Ethics in the Marketplace. Inland has won that award three times. The Chicago Association of Real estate agents has been honoring individuals with its Hall of Fame since 1883.

In 2014 Inland became the first corporation to be so honored. Inland is truly an American story. It is a company with an investor-first philosophy and Midwestern ethics. It's the heart and soul of America, what every company would want to be.

Cosenza himself is truly the product of the American Dream, his father's dream as well as his own. After Joe's father immigrated to the U.S. from Italy in 1922, he opened a barber shop in Chicago.

In the late '20s a bookie joint opened right across the street. Al Capone was the owner. Capone went to Joe's Dad for his haircuts. Joe asked his Dad if he was afraid. He was, but he still cut the mobster's hair because Capone would tip $20 on a haircut that cost 25 cents. Joe's rise to be one of the chiefs of a great American corporation had to be his father's dream for his son.

Today Joe Cosenza remembers his father fondly, the lessons he taught, and Joe honors his Dad by having his old barber's chair installed in a corner of Joe's Inland office in Oak Brook, Illinois.

Al Capone Sat Here.
Joe Cosenza's Father's Barber's Chair.

Interview with Keith Lampi
President & CEO
Inland Private Capital

The youthful president of Inland Private Capital majored in economics and minored in finance at the University of Illinois in Champaign. He says he was drawn to the financial markets and had a particular interest in real estate. He's been with Inland for 16 years:

"I took my first position at Inland kind of thinking to myself: this would be a good start, [it would] expose me to a number of things, and after a couple of months I was hooked. I realized it's so intuitive, such a dynamic asset type, one that isn't just a buy-hold-sell. It's a buy; it's a manage; it's a devote creativity-and-resources, navigating what's going on in the marketplace, what may occur, and how to deal with a lot of problem-solving. It's not a one-size-fits-all kind of proposition. There's so much going on that intrigued me that I realized real estate is where I belonged."

Tell us about the Great Recession of 2008, how that affected real estate in general and Inland in particular.

"Oh gosh, it was, from my perspective it was the first real economic downturn that I had personally faced, and that our industry had faced... The securitized 1031 market really didn't begin until the late '90s, early 2000s, and really wasn't big enough to speak to the economic volatility in the early 2000s. So, it really kind of established a footwork or foundation and grew incrementally, year over year."

"The IRS came out with guidance in 2002 that catapulted the growth of the industry. Then again in 2004 it further [enhanced] the legitimacy of the securitized 1031 market, and there was more or less vertical sales growth, demand drive from investors all the way up to about 2007, 2008. And the Great Recession hit.

"It was a recession that was deep-rooted. It was a real estate-related recession. It was a finance-related recession, and our industry all about went away. Commercial real estate broadly speaking was absolutely affected; everything was affected. There was a high degree of uncertainty early on. There were questions being asked with respect to, say are some of the major banks going to be nationalized? Concepts that are so fundamental to commercial real estate, there were such open-ended question marks. It was a scary time.

"A lot of sellers either weren't selling because they didn't like the value or weren't selling because they couldn't find a buyer willing to pay anything for their property; oftentimes the buyer couldn't finance it because there was so much uncertainty with respect to the banks. I'll say it was probably an 18-month period. We were on pretty shaky footing... Various incremental steps were taken throughout that built confidence and re-established the fact that we maybe kind of hit a bottom and were kind of coming out of that, and the industry by most accounts almost had to start over.

"I think Sponsors like Inland were forced to take a hard look in the mirror and look at what we'd done pre-recession and we could do post. That is, create products that were better positioned to weather an economic downturn or storm. So, cost structures, fee structures were looked at in very, very critical fashion. What asset types were acquired on behalf of our broader marketplace from a sector and geography standpoint, and how to better provide investors with more diversity. All of these were questions we were asking ourselves as Sponsors. Broker-dealers were asking themselves as the fiduciary on behalf of their investors, and as a result I actually think they came out better, stronger and in a better position to service their clientele."

Lampi says the industry is again on an upward trajectory, but the 2007-8 downturn is always in the back of one's mind. He says there's emphasis on putting investors in long-term vehicles that have the ability to weather an economic storm.

Long-term minded. How long are we talking about?
"I typically like our program built with a 10-year time horizon. Certainly, that could go longer. There are absolutely various examples I could cite where the holding period was shorter, depending on macroeconomic factors and what the general market was as related to opportunities or challenges. Ten years is typically what we model."

Can you give us some idea about the analytics, the software you use to evaluate a property?

"I could go on a long-winded narrative about what technology has done for markets and pockets of industries. Real estate's no different. What technology has basically done is it allows us to evaluate a larger volume of opportunities in a compressed, shorter period of time in a more thorough way.

"It's a game of numbers: the more you look at, the more opportunities you can unearth that make sense and fit the objective you ultimately want to provide investors. So, the more you can look at in a timely fashion, the better. That means from a demographic analysis standpoint, having access to technology that gives you profiles on certain markets as it relates to income and population growth and then all of the various factors you might want to see if you're buying an apartment complex, for example.

"But it doesn't stop there. There's a variety of different proprietary software systems that we'll invest in and we subscribe to that also give us intel in what the market rents are within a one-mile radius of the property we're going to acquire... How many units are being developed which may impact your ability to maintain your occupancy level or push rents. New job growth that's occurring in the area. The list goes on and on..."

Is there a trend toward more multifamily apartments?

"We're of the belief that the only way you're really going to make money in real estate on a near-term and even mid- and long-term basis if you're buying in this market environment is to purchase assets with operating characteristics.

"What that basically means is you want to buy assets that you believe you can create and add value to by rolling up your sleeves and being a solid manager of real estate by maximizing occupancy and rent growth on the income side of the equation, and shrewdly managing your expenses on the expense side of the equation. Imagine your tax increases, insurance, salaries, all the ancillary expenses that translate to your bottom line. Apartments fit that mold well. They're assets that don't manage themselves.

"Yes, it's important to buy a good asset in a well-located market but the story doesn't end there. You also have to be good at what you do in managing that asset on behalf of investors...creating that market value by being a shrewd asset manager.

Apartments really accomplish that goal for us. And we also see some of the same opportunity in student housing and self-storage and other assets…"

In the lobby of Inland Private Capital Corporation there are photographs of some of Inland's holdings, including student housing at the University of Central Florida and various medical office buildings all across the country. We asked: what's the difference between medical office buildings and other office buildings?

"The medical office arena is more of a planned demography. It's a more of a play on the healthcare sector. Corporate office space is a different animal… It's more downtown, centralized… A medical office can be successful in the surrounding suburban sprawl. Proximity to major hospital systems oftentimes play to the analysis in evaluating a medical practice that may house themselves in a medical office building.

"But really, the medical office building or MOB sector is with the demographic trend of the Baby Boomers, the aging sector… This is a play on demography which just isn't really the same thought process when you're looking at corporate office space. In fact, there's some research in suggesting that there's more transient employees, there's more of a desire to provide employees with the option to work from home that would ultimately lessen the floor plan a corporate office may need, so it really is a pretty different analysis, when all is said and done."

Property owners have different options in cashing out, including charitable remainder trusts and installment sales among others. Any thoughts?

"From a tax standpoint, clearly these are options; it's not a one-size-fits-all. Each investor has a different set of needs, desires, objectives that they aspire to accomplish. That's why it's so important for investors to work with a team of financial professionals, starting with the financial advisor… their accountants and estate planning attorneys and making sure that the decisions that are made fit within the broader objectives of the client's plan. I wouldn't sit here and suggest that one approach is better than another or makes sense …That's going to be ferreted out when a client steps back and works with a team of professionals."

Are there long and short strategies for investment properties?

"I think there can be. I would say the securitized 1031 market has been more of a long-term proposition. The marketplace hasn't really spoken to that short-term minded client who wants to park cash for a period of time and then achieve liquidity and then go do something else. That's not really what Delaware Statutory Trusts and the securitized 1031 market has been about.

"There are certain assets that may be shorter term hold propositions: an asset with shorter term financing that has perhaps a value-add proposition attached to it, probably on the higher risk side of the spectrum, but it could also be higher upside in the shorter-term hold.

"Inland has done a concept of five-year type structures. Those are more few and far between… When I explain our marketplace to people, I find using the baseball analogy [helpful]: 90% of our investors have done really well by themselves by investing actively in real estate, buying and selling, actively owning and managing their own property, and it's that point in their lives where they no longer want to be active owners, but they like real estate, they believe in it, and they obviously are tax sensitive. So, they roll their proceeds out of an actively managed property into a passive one. And they've already swung for the fences, they've already hit their homeruns, they've already accumulated a great deal of wealth and by the time they get to our industry, our marketplace, they're looking to hit consistent singles, they're looking to preserve capital, they're looking to put their money to work for them in the form of income. Because of that, a long-term mind set it makes sense."

Is there a cash reserve factor built in?
"Always, always. In fact, I preach this internally, but we go to great pains to err on the side of making sure there's even more than we believe we're going to need because the real estate industry is dynamic and you can never completely predict exactly what's going to occur. There always are surprises, some pleasant, some unpleasant, so you're better served having more cash set aside just in case."

At tax time, what sort of forms do investors get?
"If it's a DST, it's a 1099 which is a pretty simple document. It's a summary of the property level income and expenses; shows the net income translated to investors who use that to fill out

schedule E on their tax return. That's a process most of our investors are familiar with because that's how they filed for their prior holdings.

The difference is, with a DST it's all very clean, broken out and presented in a simple digestible form that most accountants can navigate pretty efficiently."

There's a perception that investors are taking their money out of multifamily units in California.

"In our industry we're still seeing the largest percentage of influx still going into apartments. Now there's certainly some geographic considerations. I think in California, for example, pricing dynamics are a bit more of an outlier when compared to national averages.

"So, we do see a lot of inflow of capital coming from the respective coasts and a lot of times those investors are observing: I can sell my property for a value that is well above what I ever thought I would get, and I can redeploy that capital into another market, a similar asset, a multi-family dwelling in a different market that maybe has more in the way of income producing potential and upside potential. That's kind of dependent on the particular market but apartments consistently are the leading sector that 1031 investors in our industry are allocating capital to. That's at the moment. That tide can absolutely change."

What about the Amazon Effect?
"It goes back to that discussion we had earlier about technology...Inland in its retail strategy has for several years now really dedicated its pursuit of new opportunities and isolated them into grocery-anchored facilities and facilities that have a large concentration in service-related [establishments]: nail salons, and haircuts and establishments that can't be bought online.

"It was a hedge against the online phenomenon, but even taking that approach doesn't isolate you, doesn't make you immune to what's going on and how retailers are impacted. Retailers conclude that maybe they need less space than before. We've seen it already this year with Sports Authority, for example. Retailers are put out of business as a result.

"What that's creating is more available space which translates into downward pressure on rents which can affect your values. I think the retail industry will emerge and kind of process its way through the Amazon Effect, and long term, I think buying a well-located shopping center and having a long-term mindset can make a high degree of sense. But it's definitely an inflection point for that particular sector, and one you really need to navigate with caution."

There certainly are Other Formidable DST Sponsors

"Yes, Inland stands above the rest of the DST Sponsors in capital raise numbers but it would not be fair not to mention others. There are seven or eight formidable newcomers to the field, that are snapping at the heels of Inland."

INTERVIEW WITH WARREN THOMAS, FOUNDING PARTNER EXCHANGERIGHT

ExchangeRight of Pasadena, California, is the third largest provider of DSTs in the industry, with more than $2 billion of property under management.

The company was formed in 2012 in the aftermath of the Great Recession. Founders Warren Thomas, Joshua Ungerecht, and David Fisher had the idea of creating a 1031 Exchangeable product for investors that would withstand the next inevitable downturn in the economy. Their philosophy was and is to protect their investors' capital and the stability of their income.

Geoff Flahardy was working at another real estate company during the 2008 recession. When he heard about ExchangeRight and its philosophy, he joined the company in order to help build out its DST platform. Geoff Flahardy is another one of the real pioneers in the DST industry as well, seeing its value to the investor and its tremendous potential early on.

His dedication to the industry and investors is truly remarkable. His ethics and core business values are to the highest standards. Add that to his tremendous technical skills in analyzing transactions making sense out of seemingly complicated and complex issues and you have a person who is in the right place at the right time taking care of business. Professional from the word "go" he is known for his straight talk and is never in a selling mode. "Just the facts ma'am."

His business career started when he was finishing work on his college degree in Organizational Communication. He posted his resume on a jobs board and was hired as an intern in 2001 and became a full-time employee six months later. When the company launched a subsidiary to offer Tenant-in-Common investments, Geoff became one of their specialists in 1031 Exchanges.

As with other DST issuers, ExchangeRight follows a number of detailed steps in forming the Trust, Private Placement Memorandum creation, getting third party tax opinion and so forth. Geoff took notice of corporate

NNN properties that held up well in 2008-2010. We asked Warren Thomas of ExchangeRight to share with us their reasoning behind certain decisions that they made in developing their business. The answers were fascinating.

Why did you form ExchangeRight Securities, LLC in 2012?

"The founding partners of ExchangeRight formed the company to meet the needs of their personal investors who were seeking to complete 1031 Exchanges and desired property assets that could preserve capital and deliver reliable monthly income, regardless of the economic conditions that might accompany a recession or economic turmoil. ExchangeRight introduced the 1031 DST industry to multi-property portfolios of net-leased assets with long-term leases guaranteed by investment grade corporation. The ExchangeRight model incorporated the use of modest levels of debt with high to very high debt-service coverage ratios, to protect the investor and the portfolio from defaults and risk of foreclosure. ExchangeRight also introduced the concept of waiving certain disposition fees while providing a strategically planned exit of aggregated portfolios. The result of this model was that ExchangeRight has issued 32 net leased portfolios, all with returns meeting or exceeding original projections and now manages total assets of $2.4B."

In both the investment and exit strategy, why is ExchangeRight taking the current approach?

"We have taken the approach of building portfolios of net leased assets that have been first and foremost generating consistent cash flow with little to no risk of losing capital due to debt structure that could result in future foreclosure risk. Secondly, we are targeting future exits that allow our portfolios to be aggregated and command a premium through sales to institutional and high net worth buyers. We are quite pleased that our portfolio approach has resulted in each DST meeting or exceeding original projections in their operations. We are also very encouraged in our early talks with our investment bankers on our future DST exits."

Why is ExchangeRight focused on retail assets?

"ExchangeRight is focused on retail net leased assets that we expect to perform well in challenging economic conditions. These types of assets have experienced strong retail performance during the prior recession and we expect them to do the same should economic conditions worsen. We buy the assets we buy because they are naturally defensive in nature because of the products and markets they serve as well as because of the credit of the corporations that tenant the properties."

Are you concerned about the Amazon Effect?

"We watch for the Amazon Effect with every asset type that we purchase. Although we are always concerned, we concentrate on necessity-based retail asset types that have thus far had very little impact from Amazon. Auto part retailers, medical providers, pharmacy, dollar stores, Tractor Supply, banks and our other specialized retailers have gained market shares often because of their focus on discount and necessity items that are not as easily or as timely available from Amazon."

What is your outlook for the economy and real estate markets?

"We are hopeful that current tax, economic and regulatory policies will continue to prolong economic growth, but we know the economy is overdue for both a correction and recession. Recession will challenge both occupancies and rent levels of many real estate asset types. Therefore, we continue to acquire net lease assets with investment grade tenants that we expect will perform well in a recessionary environment.

"We also will continue to seek multifamily assets, but we will only acquire those assets that have a significant value add component which can assist the property to retain and increase in value during tough economic times."

CANTOR FITZGERALD

Cantor Fitzgerald is a global financial services firm and was founded in 1945. There are 10,000 employees in 60 offices in 20 countries spread-out over-all corners of the globe operating under the Cantor Fitzgerald umbrella of companies and affiliates.

After Cantor Fitzgerald lost 658 employees tragically in the September 11, 2001 terrorist attack in New York City, CEO Howard Lutnick vowed to keep the company alive. Its trading markets were back online within a week and the company also vowed to give 25% of its profits over the next five years to the families of the employees who were killed.

Cantor Fitzgerald's DST business comprises single tenant and multi-family properties. To learn more about this great company please watch their video or check them out on line at www.cantor.com

Accommodator's Perspective, Your 1031 Exchange Escrow: Interview with William Exeter, President & CEO Exeter 1031

I sat down with one of the leaders in the 1031 Exchange space: Bill Exeter. William L. Exeter is President and Chief Executive Officer for Exeter 1031 Exchange Services, LLC, Exeter IRA Services, LLC and their affiliate companies.

Building and Maintaining Wealth
"Real estate investors spend a lifetime buying, building and managing their investment real estate portfolio, but they rarely consider what they will do once they get to the point where they are "done" with managing their investment real estate."

"The sale of investment real estate will generally result in the recognition of federal and state ordinary income, capital gain and/or depreciation recapture tax liabilities. It may also trigger the Medicare ("Obamacare") Surcharge. The combined federal and state income tax paid can easily approach 40% of the investor's taxable gain."

"Payment of these income tax liabilities will significantly reduce the amount of equity (cash) available to reinvest in other rental, investment or business use properties thus making it extremely difficult for an investor to continue building his or her wealth."

"Investors are often very good at building and creating wealth through the accumulation of an investment real estate portfolio, but keeping that wealth is just as important as building it. Why work so hard to build your wealth if you lose a large percentage of that wealth to taxes?"

Planning Your Exit Strategy

"Investors, in conjunction with their legal, tax and financial advisors, should start planning as early as possible for their 'exit strategy' by answering questions such as: Do I want to change my investment real estate portfolio in any way? Do I need more cash flow instead of appreciation for my retirement? Do I want to reduce the amount of time that I spend on property management activities? Do I want to spend my wealth or leave it to my kids and/or grandkids? There are many other factors that an investor may want to consider when contemplating an exit strategy, which is why working with legal, tax and financial advisors is exceptionally important."

"Tax deferral strategies can effectively allow an investor to reposition or rebalance his/her investment real estate portfolio to accomplish any number of financial, tax or estate planning goals and objectives while deferring the payment of federal, and in most cases, state income tax liabilities."

"One of the most popular tax-deferral strategies today is the tax-deferred exchange pursuant to Section 1031 of the Internal Revenue Code ("1031 Exchange")."

1031 Exchange

"The 1031 Exchange allows an investor to sell appreciated rental, investment or business use real estate and defer the payment of income tax liabilities as long as he/she remains fully invested by acquiring Qualified Use and like-kind replacement real estate of equal or greater value."

"Structuring a 1031 Exchange is certainly an excellent transaction tool for deferring the payment of taxes when an investor sells rental or investment real estate. However, the 1031 Exchange is much, much more than just a transaction tool. It is an incredible wealth building opportunity. It allows the investor to continually defer the payment of capital gain and depreciation recapture income tax liabilities over his/her lifetime. This means that investors can continue exchanging properties as a life-long strategy, always deferring the payment of their income tax liabilities and keeping their equity (cash) working for them. This strategy allows investors to significantly increase the value of their investment real estate portfolio and consequently their net worth over their lifetime."

"It can also be a tax elimination strategy. An investor can continually defer the payment of income tax liabilities through a life-long 1031 Exchange strategy, and then leave the investment real estate to heirs who will receive a step-up and cost basis thereby completely eliminating the payment of any capital gain and depreciation recapture taxes."

Qualified Intermediary

"You will need a professional, experienced, knowledgeable and financially sound Qualified Intermediary like Exeter 1031 Exchange Services, LLC to structure your 1031 Exchange transaction. The Qualified Intermediary is responsible for the administration of your 1031 Exchange transaction, including (1) preparation of your 1031 Exchange documents; and, (2) safeguarding your 1031 Exchange funds; and (3) consulting with you and your advisors regarding the implementation of your 1031 Exchange transaction."

Qualified Use Requirement

"One of the most important issues regarding 1031 Exchanges is the Qualified Use requirement. In other words, what types of property qualify for 1031 Exchange treatment?"

"Investors often get hung up on how long they have held or will hold title to real estate in order to determine if they qualify for 1031 Exchange treatment. There is no holding period requirement. The actual requirement is that under audit the investor must be able to demonstrate the intent to hold the relinquished property and their replacement property for rental, investment or business use."

"The longer the investor holds the subject properties for investment purposes the easier it is to prove the intent was to hold for rental, investment or business use. However, if an investor has a short-term holding period, he might still be able to qualify if he can satisfactorily demonstrate that he did have the intent to hold but there were either business, economic or other reasons for the short-term hold."

"Property held for sale by rehabbers, flippers, developers, and building contractors generally will not qualify for 1031 Exchange treatment because they bought the property with the intent to rehab, improve or build and then sell. It is treated as inventory in their real estate business. Property acquired for personal use such as your primary residence, second home or vacation property will not qualify unless changes are made regarding the usage of the property."

Like-Kind Property Requirement
"There is a lot of misinformation circulating today

about the Like-Kind Property requirement. It does not mean that you must buy a condo if you sell a condo. It only means that you are selling real estate and must therefore buy real estate. It is a very broad definition – real estate for real estate – period."

1031 Exchange Deadlines

"Investors must comply with very specific deadlines in order to qualify for 1031 Exchange treatment, including the 45 calendar-day identification requirement and the 180 calendar-day exchange deadline. These deadlines both start running upon the closing of the sale of the relinquished property. There is no extension available for these deadlines. The 45 calendar-day identification requirement can be very stressful when you are trying to locate and identify property to acquire as part of your 1031 Exchange transaction."

"One of the many benefits of identifying and acquiring a beneficial interest in a Delaware Statutory Trust ("DST") as part of a 1031 Exchange is that you can substantially eliminate the risk of the 45 calendar-day identification period by purchasing and closing on one or more DSTs during the 45 calendar-day period."

"Investors often identify DST investment properties as back-up properties or to be used with any excess 1031 Exchange funds that are left over after the acquisition of their target property."

Identifying Replacement Properties
"Potential replacement properties must be identified to the 1031 Exchange Qualified Intermediary within the 45 calendar-day identification period. The property identification should be specific and must comply with either the three (3) property rule, the 200% of fair market value rule, or the 95% exception. Basically, the three-property rule is to identify no more than 3 replacement properties and close on between one and three of them in the allotted 180 days. Another option is the 200% FMV rule. This rule allows an investor to identify as many properties as they like as long as the combined fair market value of those properties does not exceed 200% of the investors relinquished property sale price. And finally, the 95% rule allows an investor to identify as many properties as they like as long as the investor actually acquires and closes on 95% of them."

Refer to your 1031 escrow company for details or an accommodator. Here are a couple of excellent sources: www.EXETER1031.com www.IPX1031.com.

Reinvestment Requirement

"The value of the replacement properties acquired must be equal to or greater than the value of the relinquished properties sold. In other words, the investor must trade equal or up in value based upon the relinquished property value. You are not just reinvesting the profit or the equity, but the entire value."

"The investor can certainly complete a 'partial 1031 Exchange' by trading down in value and/or pulling some equity (cash) out of the 1031 Exchange transaction, but it will result in the recognition of taxable gain. There is no way to pull cash out without incurring tax consequences."

"You can sell multiple relinquished properties and or acquire multiple replacement properties as part of either a consolidation or a diversification strategy. The DST can be a huge help when investors want to diversify their investment real estate portfolio."

Q&A WITH THE LEADING DST MONEY GUY: CONVERSATION WITH CHARLES JENSEN

Charles Jensen, Senior Vice President Inland Securities Corporation. Charles is called the leading capital raiser on DSTs in the nation and this is what he shared with me on the topic of DSTs.

Charles, why is the DST industry growing, what do you attribute this to?

"I attribute this growth to the demographic changes happening in the United States. When you look at our population and the areas that we are growing in, the Baby Boomer aspect of that group is growing significantly right now; They are 25% of the population. They want the tax benefits of the 1031

Exchange, but they don't want the hassle of the day-to-day management. The Delaware Statutory Trust has many benefits. Some of these benefits are the diversification they get because of the multiple properties inside of one Delaware Statutory Trust.

"The management is fully taken care of for them so there's no "tenants, toilets, trash, terminal termites, teenagers, taxes" and they get professional management in high-quality properties. The minimum is only $100,000 and just like a typical 1031 Exchange investors are allowed to "swap until they drop" as we say in the industry. The seniors can exchange over and over again, and upon death there's a "step-up in cost basis" to their heirs, [i.e.: they will not have capital gains on the appreciated value.] So, this is a really interesting way to own real estate without the hassles of management."

"To be in high quality properties with a nice income stream some seniors think about creating a charitable trust, but what they can do is look into a Delaware Statutory Trust instead. DSTs send out a monthly income, and also have a growth potential. The person that would like to set up a charitable remainder trust, can instead set up a Delaware Statutory Trust and actually take the income while they're alive. Then upon death, have the income and the property inherited over to the charity with a charitable remainder trust.

"Instead of giving control over to the charity while alive, being in a Delaware Statutory Trust allows you to remain in control of the asset but not the day-to-day operations. The great thing about the Delaware Statutory Trust is that when it completes and goes full cycle or sells, you have the option of rolling that money into another exchange and starting over again, almost like Groundhog Day."

Charles, as the industry is now matured, and investors are more familiar with the DST concept, you were saying that you're seeing very large investors choosing DST for their Exchange as well, is this correct?... Why are the larger investors that seem to have options, doing DSTs?

"Just like smaller investors, larger investors have similar goals with regard to retirement. They not only want to retire from their job, but also retire from the management of their properties. Last year in Los Angeles, my average size of a DST was $600,000. [This claim can be made of previous years as well.] I believe the wealthy investors are realizing that the Delaware Statutory Trust is a viable option. Now we're also seeing even larger deals, in the $10–20, $50 million range.

"Typically, if an investor has over $15 million in equity, we can offer up a customized 1031 Exchange instead of being in the Delaware Statutory Trust with 500 investors. If they have over $15 million, they can go into a customized 1031 Exchange through Inland. We are one of the few DST firms in the nation that allows for customized exchanges. This allows the investors to remain in control of the decisions but allows Inland to do the property management on a big asset. The other reason large investors like to work with Delaware Statutory Trusts is the idea of diversification."

"We recently worked with a very wealthy group of families in a trust in Hawaii. They had many properties destroyed by hurricanes in the 1990s which affected the cash flow on their trust. They decided it would be best to convert certain properties into a Delaware Statutory Trust on the mainland managed by Inland. They now have diversification from geographical issues such as hurricanes, and higher quality properties with professional management from Inland with very little day-to-day operations at all on the properties. There's no management they have to spend time on, they're also getting a higher cash flow than they were receiving on the Hawaiian Islands.

"In addition, they are getting a lower "property management see-through." Inland is diversified into multiple states and multiple asset classes. For example, they were getting charged 12% on the rents on their properties in the Hawaiian Islands, and Inland is only charging 3% on the rents anyway so not only did the property management fee go down drastically, but their income went up as well."

"One of the interesting things about a 1031 Exchange is the fact that if you have a million-dollar property you need to replace a million dollars in real estate to be fully tax-deferred. Now if you have a property that has leverage this gets a little more complicated, so if you had a million-dollar property and it was $500,000 in debt and $500,000 in equity you have a 50% loan to value. When you sold this property the $500,000 in debt was paid back to the original bank regional loan, thus leaving you with $500,000 in proceeds. But the issue is $500,000 does not replace the full million on the replacement property. This requires individuals to get another loan for the $500,000 or to come out of pocket with the $500,000 to replace the debt.

"The problem is that most investors don't have $500,000 laying around so they are forced to get another loan to replace the debt in a DST. With the allowed up to 500 investors, it is too difficult to get 500 people approved for a loan, so we take out one loan on the property and investors absorb our debt. Some of our deals have zero debt; some have 50% loan to value; and some have 60% loan to value or higher. The fact that you don't need to get another loan simplifies the process. One of the important things to realize in a Delaware Statutory Trust is that all the properties are pre-closed and pre-financed and all due diligence is completed in advance for us, making it turn key to the investor."

"This turn key solution is almost like picking out items from a menu at a restaurant, you can look at the different DSTs to see which ones matches your objectives. Choose between one company or many or pre-select the best of three."

"Our acquisitions process is very robust; we look at many states. We look at states that are growing, industries that are growing, and we try to focus on areas that provide necessities in the market such as apartments, storage units. In medical facilities we looked through hundreds and literally thousands of properties to find that one property to go into the DST. Sometimes if you go to your local real estate agent or commercial real estate broker, they farm a certain area of town.

"For example, if you go to San Diego, they'll show you San Diego properties in San Diego markets such as Temecula. Typically, that local broker will not show you a national portfolio. But Inland is practically looking at properties in almost every state in the nation, and we like states that are the path of growth."

Tell us about some of the other major rewards in dealing with DSTs that you've experienced.
"Clearly the Delaware Statutory Trust is not for everyone, but for the people that this does fit, it's an amazing experience. I have met with investors who own multiple apartment buildings and have done all the management themselves; to see the stress in their faces and hear it in their voices is heartbreaking. I've had some closing dinners months after the investor has invested in a DST. To see their face, and how they look now...; they are in a state of tranquility

because their tenants are no longer calling them about a water heater or an issue in the middle of the night. Many are rested and seem able to have a higher quality of life. Nothing makes me happier than helping people realize their goals objectives and live a better life."

"We have begun working with a lot of commercial brokers and residential real estate agents. We have realized there's a lot of synergies between what we do and what they do. Sometimes an investor is retired and doesn't have an income, so he or she can't qualify for a loan. Or sometimes an investor's credit is hurt from a divorce or some life event. The Delaware Statutory Trust doesn't require a credit score for the investor because Inland arranges the debt and Inland Services the debt.

"So, when many real estate agents or commercial brokers have a situation where the investor is turned down for financing on their 1031 Exchange, they can turn to the financial advisor for the financing through the DST. Not only to replace the debt, but also under the three- property rule the real estate agent can put it on his property as #2 and 3, as a backup behind the real estate broker. Or they can work in coordination with a Delaware Statutory

Trust and a real piece of property. The Delaware Statutory Trust has allowed many real estate agents to get many more listings because we're bringing this solution to the table. To the aging Baby Boomers and many others in addition, the DST provides properties that are off market to real estate agents, thus allowing investors a larger choice of properties nationwide."

Former PricewaterhouseCooper Senior Corporate Auditor/CPA "Voice of the Industry" Mark Kosanke

Let me introduce you to an early pioneer of the DST industry: Mark Kosanke, CPA. The former PricewaterhouseCooper Senior Corporate Auditor, who was instrumental in creating the first trade association now called Alternative and Direct Investment Association (ADISA). He is past president and board member of 14 years.

In my opinion, Kosanke was a great 'get' for this book, as he is widely thought of and respected as the voice of this industry. It is my hope that you the reader, if you don't have already, will now get a laser focused understanding of just exactly what a DST can do for you, your life style, your business, and your legacy. I now give you Mark Kosanke:

"As a CPA, what I am telling clients about 1031/DSTs...

"Bob Seger, one of my favorite artists, has a song called "The Famous Final Scene." Perhaps he wasn't speaking about death but a 1031 Exchange strategy. For years tax accountants, investments advisors and CPAs have encouraged their clients to utilize their employers' 401k, 403b, IRAs and other tax deferred accounts. They are great tools. but with one caveat. Someday someone will pay tax on the monies in those funds. They will pay tax on all the money contributed along with all the growth earned over the years. So, whether it is the contributor paying on his/her own withdrawals, or beneficiaries paying on inherited qualified money, the tax will get paid someday.

"So how is a 1031 Exchange different? A 1031 allows for deferral of the gain today. Much like an IRA allows for the deferral today of current income. But subsequent 1031s allow for continued deferral, and another, and another until, I like to say, that you have maximized your tax deferral strategy. How do you maximize the strategy? You die! That's right.

Die. The adage in our business is 'swap until you drop!' So, what happens after I drop?

"An IRA and a 1031 Exchange operate very differently from a tax standpoint. In an IRA, our beneficiaries inherit our qualified funds and the associated taxes on them. In the case of inherited assets, like real estate and stocks, the rules are entirely different. Our beneficiaries (spouses, children, significant others) inherit those assets from us at the fair market value on the date of our death. So, while you as the deferring party may have little to no tax basis, and therefore huge gains, the beneficiaries' basis becomes market value on the date of death. Sale immediately following death results in no tax! The deferred tax goes "poof" on the exchanger's last breath.

"For example, say you have a property worth $1M with a $100,000 basis. You have a $900,000 taxable gain. If you sell the property on Friday and do not complete a 1031 Exchange, you will owe taxes on the entire gain, a roughly $200,000 tax bill depending on the state you live in. If instead you die on Thursday night before closing, and your children sell the property following Monday's funeral, they have zero taxes to pay. Why? Because their tax basis "stepped up" when you died. Their tax basis is $1M.

Their sale is completely tax free. The entire tax bill went "poof!"

"So, if you are someone who has been utilizing an IRA, 401k, 403b or other similar account to defer taxes you should view a 1031 Exchange as the ultimate tax deferral tool. Qualified accounts on steroids. And one of the best wealth transferring tools there is. It's a final scene worth planning for!"

The final scene as reality

"I work with a lot of clients who feel their final scene is always a-long-ways away. They manage their properties, work with the tenants, the contractors, the leasing agents, the local authorities. They have it down. They are maximizing the income and value of the real estate. Their spouse or children on the other hand are clueless. If all of a sudden, because of death, the management of the properties fell into their laps it would be chaos.

"In many cases the properties are sold by surviving beneficiaries at bargain prices because a) they just want the cash, b) they have no idea how to manage the property, c) they live out of the area and don't want to be bothered, or d) have no clue what the real value of the real estate is. I've seen many examples where a hardworking, dedicated owner passes away unexpectedly. The resulting sales are a fraction of what that aging owner could have sold those properties for if he had committed to an orderly sale, maximizing their values, and exchanging into a professionally managed, high quality real estate, providing market income without the worry of management."

A better Curtain-call

"Sometimes the hardest part for personal owners/ managers of real estate is letting go. Most of these entrepreneurs have been accumulating, developing, and managing for decades. It's just not in their DNA to stop. In the end, the reality is that what has been built over those long hard years of work is best retained and passed on to future generations by letting go. Letting go and putting the future in the hands of a nationally experienced, industry-dedicated professional team. By planning and executing an orderly transition to these real estate professionals the sweat equity of years is retained, and more importantly, passed on to their heirs, tax free using the 1031 Exchange.

"One of the objections to this approach is the "I don't need a partner." Individual owners look at various exit strategies involving multiple co-owners, like a Delaware Statutory Trust (DST), as a threat to their style, an added burden of dealing with other people, a loss of control. While that is one side of the equation, the other side is much more important. The other side is a national real estate company, encompassing in some cases billions of dollars in real estate, and looking to maximize owner value at every turn.

"The properties bought through a DST are far superior than what the average investor is ever going to have the chance to afford or buy. The tenants will be bigger, stronger, more credit worthy that anything an individual investor can hope for. The properties most likely are newer and better located. In some cases, multiple properties will be combined into one DST offering greater diversification than an individual could ever hope for. The DST Sponsor also handles all the communication. There are generally no dealings ever with the other co-owners (beneficiaries) in the DST. You may not want a partner, but if that partner has expertise and reaches far beyond your own doesn't it make sense let them do what they do best.

"The DST Sponsors are charged with the task of providing monthly "mailbox" income that can be relied upon by you in retirement. Ultimately, upon your passing, your beneficiaries continue to enjoy that same monthly income that continues to flow without any effort on their part. What a passing gift that is. Your wife, your children, continue to get the same income you were generating without the need to deal with the toilets, the tenants, or the trash. It's a curtain call that deserves a bow as you have provided the ultimate performance for your loved one!

"I have a 76-year-old client who has been 'hands on' in managing 24 beautiful single-family rentals. He meticulously maintains them, handles the tenants, deals with the city inspectors, and works with the various contractors. His wife has never even seen the inside of half of the properties even though they are all within 30 minutes of their residence. His two daughters live in other states. He nets about 2% cash flow on the value of the assets.

"If something untimely were to happen to him what do you suppose would happen to the real estate? Most likely his wife/daughters would liquidate, stopping the flow of income. How long would that take? Perhaps years. And without personal knowledge of the real estate, perhaps at sale prices below true value. Smartly, this client has been slowly selling and transitioning these properties, via a 1031 Exchange and DST, into "mailbox" income that his wife and daughter can enjoy beyond his curtain call."

Hey Good Lookin'

"Hey Good Lookin', whatcha got cookin'?" So says Jimmy Buffet. Well who are these DST Sponsors and why should we trust them with our lifetime of accumulated wealth?

These are companies like Inland Private Capital, who you've read about in other places in this book. Companies with a national presence. Companies with entire acquisition and disposition departments. Companies with insurance departments, property tax appeal departments, and management departments. Companies that look at 100 properties before buying one. There is little doubt that investing in a DST with one of these Sponsors will mean you will have a better property, better tenant, better location, and more upside than anything you could ever buy on your own. The depth and experience of their nationally staffed departments is unparalleled.

"Imagine taking your local knowledge and spreading it across the entire country. That's what you are getting with a DST Sponsor. Imagine a whole department dedicated to reducing taxes, reducing loan rates, competitively bidding out services, negotiating leases. Why buy local when you can buy, via a DST, into the strongest growing market in the country. In a state where there may be no state or local taxes. In a state where demand is growing. In a new property with no barriers to entry to the locale. The average individual investor just can't touch the kind of real estate offered in a DST.

"DSTs offer extremely competitive, on a net return basis, returns. In my experience, most clients think they are getting an 8-10% return on their assets. In reality, with few exceptions, the total net return I see on many tax returns is far less and averages about 3% on true net value. DSTs by comparison may offer a far more consistent return at a higher overall rate. And without the worry of management. A good lookin' return!

"DSTs offer so much more. The typical investor has some level of debt on their property. In most cases that debt carries personal guarantees. Can the individual investor hope to negotiate the same debt terms as a national DST Sponsor? DSTs offer investors the benefit of no personal guarantees. No credit checks. No tax returns, financial statements, no reporting. This is a strong estate planning tool as well. What if there is no debt? Should a seller/exchanger consider adding debt before sale? Absolutely. Debt, and therefore equity, taken out before an exchange is tax free. Debt properly structured prior to a sale allows the seller to extract equity, tax free, prior to sale. Most DSTs offer 45-55% debt leverage. By matching, or closely matching, the ending debt, the seller is able to take out equity tax free before a sale or exchange."

This makes the combination of a DST and a pre-debt extraction the most powerful tool in the 1031 Exchange handbook.

"Most investors have used refinancing over the years to maximize their real estate purchases. A DST is no different. DSTs provide the debt typically needed to complete a 1031 Exchange under IRS rules. In some cases, it provides more debt than is needed. In those cases, the opportunity exists to use the DSTs nonrecourse debt to take out tax-free equity 'locked in' our properties. Just another example of making DSTs 'good looking!!'

"Let's look at another example. Suppose my property is worth a $1M. I have about $250K (25%) of personally guaranteed debt on it. The DST I am considering is 55% leveraged. I can go and borrow

25-30% of new debt prior to sale to 'equalize' the approximate debt of the relinquished property with the replacement property. In this way I take out $250-$300K tax free before my sale. As long as I am using those funds for business or investment purposes The IRS allows this in the normal course of business."

You're my Best Friend

"The rock group Queen had a song in the 80s called 'You're My Best Friend.' So, what is the best friend of real estate investors? Depreciation! That's right. That IRS rule that allows us to offset our cash income with a non-cash deduction call depreciation. And when you combine depreciation with the tax deferring attributes of a 1031 Exchange the affect is mind blowing.

"Let's take a closer look at depreciation and a 1031. If I buy an apartment building for $1M, I can depreciate it for 27.5 years. That means, for tax purposes, I get to deduct about $36,000+ off my cash income each year. My property produces $50,000 of income after expenses.

"After deducting $36K in depreciation I pay tax on only $14K of income. A great tax sheltering reason for owning investment real estate. Now suppose I sell that property after 10 years and do not complete a 1031 Exchange. Under current tax rules I owe what's called 'recapture tax' on the $360,000 in total depreciation I took over the 10 years. I would owe $90,000 in recapture tax even if the property had not appreciated in value. It's basically the IRS saying you got to take that deduction each year, but your property didn't really depreciate, so you owe us the tax back on all those depreciation deductions you took. Recapture tax is 25% of the depreciation previously taken. This is also a major item that many investors do not take into account when 'ball parking' the tax they'll owe if they sell their property and do not complete a 1031.

"When completing a 1031 Exchange that recapture tax is not paid. And if you swap again, it's not paid again. Again, and again until death you depart. In the end, with proper planning, that recapture tax is never paid and all those deductions you took over all those years remain tax sheltered income to you for life. Just like your best friend for life!

"How can a DST help me maximize my depreciation deduction and overall income sheltering? DSTs carry leverage ranging from 0% – 80% leverage, with most in the 45% to 55% range.

Let's look at some tax planning here. If I sell my $1M property that has 30% leverage (debt) I net $700,000 in equity proceeds to exchange. If I go into an average DST with average leverage of 50%, my $700,000 buys $1.4M of new real estate. I just bought $400,000 more in real estate then I sold. I get to depreciate $400,000 more in 'additional' real estate. I just created $10-$14K more in depreciation to tax shelter my income than I had before.

"Even if my cash flow is the same, I just increased my true after-tax return by sheltering more of the income with depreciation. And, if planned properly, I will never pay tax on that additional depreciation that I am deducting each year I own my DST. This is where utilizing the DST leverage properly can create even more after-tax income than I could ever hope to create on my own.

"In comparing DSTs, you can't just look at first year cash flow. This is a mistake many investors make. You have to consider the amount of leverage. You also have to consider the type of property and the amount of depreciation that it will create. Debt reduction and amortization are also key components to consider when comparing various DSTs.

"The ability of the DST Sponsors to structure competitive debt and perform depreciation maximizing cost segregation analysis is far above even the most, savvy real estate investor, but keep in mind that additional leverage can also mean more risk."

"How do I know if he really loves me?"
"There are a myriad of DST Sponsors out there. How do I know which one is right for me? Which one has my best interest in mind? Which one will be here through good times, and in tough times? Who is just trying to make a quick buck?

"The first thing to understand is federal securities law. Basically, anytime more than a few (often defined as 5) are joined in a profit-making venture requiring the raising of capital, the sale of interests (capital) comes under federal securities law. Further, in these cases, you are now selling a 'security' and by certain disclosure rules. Unfortunately, in the real estate world this is seldom followed and hard to police. There are many examples all over the internet of companies selling "interest" in real estate without the proper disclosures and ignoring the securities laws which have been implemented to protect investors.

"Enter your licensed investment representative. Investment representatives are securities licensed and only deal with DSTs that have taken the care to go through proper channels and scrutiny. Investment representatives are further licensed through a "Broker/Dealer". For example, a real estate agent has to be licensed through a Broker. If I am a real estate agent, I am licensed through Century 21, Remax, or any other Broker. Investment advisors have to be similarly licensed through a Securities Broker/Dealer. The big names you hear are Morgan Stanley, Raymond James, Merrill Lynch and others.

"Most independent representatives specializing in the 1031 arena are licensed with smaller Broker/Dealers that specialize in this area. Broker/ Dealers bring an important function to the DST process. As DST Sponsors "offer" their programs and products out to the investment world, the Broker/Dealer assumes the role of gatekeeper. It is the responsibility of the Broker/ Dealer to review each and every DST presented to them. Only after a thorough review, and the satisfaction of questions or concerns, does a Broker/Dealer sign a 'selling agreement' whereby it begins to allow its licensed investment representatives to offer those DST programs to their clients.

"This is a huge and very important piece of investing in a DST. The scrutiny that goes into each program is far above the non-securitized transaction being pushed on the internet. There are also very active third party 'due diligence' firms that provide independent reports to the Broker/Dealer community on each program. These third-party due diligence firms provide a valuable service in highlighting potential issues and mitigating attributes within the DST.

"In the end, the DST that your investment representative is offering to retail clients has been reviewed by independent third-party due diligence firms, has been further scrutinized by the Broker/Dealers Due diligence officer, and finally reviewed as appropriate for you, the investing client. This is likely a far more, lengthy and involved process then any non-securitized offering can provide.

"The result of all this effort is that your independent representative is presenting to you DST 1031 programs that have gone through an exhaustive process to assure, as best they can, that what you are investing in is a viable offering that meets your needs and protects you as an investor."

"'R-E-S-P-E-C-T,' Aretha Franklin sings. In this industry who brings this all together to get the

RESPECT for the time, effort and talent that goes into making this industry great? The answer – ADISA. ADISA is the Alternative and Direct Investment Securities Association. This is an association made up of the top Sponsors, due diligence firms, broker dealers and representatives in the industry. This cohesive group takes the investors interest to the next level. ADISA's primary role is representing the Alternative Investment Industry and providing education, networking, and advocacy. ADISA holds three major conferences each year. These conferences provide a place to properly educate the investment professional, through a series of sessions, specifically aimed at various topics relevant to the products represented. It gives everyone in the industry a chance to network amongst peers to create better products, flow of information, and provide open discussion of industry "best practices."

"ADISA is also actively involved in monitoring new legislation that may impact the alternative investment industry. This is particularly important in tax saving vehicles like the 1031 exchange, which are constantly viewed as a potential revenue source by Congress. Since the advent of the 1031 exchange in 1921, the code has only been modified 6 times, and many of those modifications enhanced the ability to utilize 1031 exchanges. A recent example is that personal property assets starting in 2018 are no longer eligible for 1031 exchanges. This is part of the new tax law. During those Congressional discussions, ADISA, along with other real estate trade groups, actively lobbied and educated members as to the benefits of keeping 1031 for real estate in place. As a result, 1031 exchanges for real estate was retained while 1031 exchanges for other non-real assets were not. This was a great example of how this industry stays ahead of the curve in protecting the industry and its investors. Know that ADISA will continue to be a strong voice representing the interest of taxpayers and the industry alike."

"**Easy like Sunday Morning!** That's what reporting a 1031 exchange on your tax return is. As a CPA, I appreciate the fact that 1031 exchanges are definitely not an everyday strategy that is used by most of our clients. For that reason, many accountants discount the use of a 1031 merely because they haven't been exposed to it and feel the reporting is complex. In reality the reporting of a 1031 exchange is no more difficult than most other taxable transactions on a tax return."

"There are two pieces to consider here. First there is the 1031 exchange itself which is reported one time, in the year of the exchange. The reporting is similar to reporting capital gains with the caveat that the gain is being "deferred" to future years. Think of it as a carryforward if you will. And tax returns are filled with carryforward items from instalment sales, charitable contributions, capital losses, etc. Once reported, the "deferred gain" is set unless or until a subsequent sale is completed and a 1031 exchange is not utilized."

"Secondly, there is the reporting of the DST income. When investing in a DST the end result is that I am a "beneficial owner" of the DST. The IRS considers the DST to be a "pass through" entity for tax purposes. What does all that mean? It means I report my DST income in the exact same place I report any rental income property that I have. That place is the Schedule E for individual taxpayers. The Sponsors do an excellent job of reporting the total income of the DST properties and then breaking down each beneficial owner's percentages for reporting purposes. Sponsors provide concise, easy to understand year end reports that make the reporting of these income properties extremely efficient."

"The Beach Boys sing, '**Wouldn't it be nice**.' Well, yes, it would be. Let's look at some real-life examples of transactions I have been involved in that changed the lives of the people I worked with."

"I had a couple in their mid-60's who were managing a 100+ unit aging apartment complex. They were sweet as can be. And they loved their renters and knew most of them well. So nice and sweet were they that they hardly ever wanted to raise their rents. As a result, they were able to take about $6,000 a month of income from the property. Which they thought was great. But along came a buyer offering them $4M for the property. Because their basis was near zero it also meant nearly a $1M tax bill. Enter the 1031 and a DST. By utilizing the 1031 exchange they we able to put the entire $4M in proceeds to work for them.

"The DSTs they invested in resulted in creating income of over $16,000 per month. This was a life changing event for this couple. They were able to retire, substantially increase their net spendable income, and focus on their health. In the first year they bought a second home in Florida and enjoyed the first cruise of their life. Never did they dream that the asset they toiled at could be used to transform their life and now have the opportunity to enjoy their retirement years. It was a great example of stopping yourself, looking at your situation, and realizing that it was time for the asset to work for you and not the other way around."

"This is typical of compassionate, commendable people who manage real estate with emotions instead of for higher profit. This is where the professionalism of the DST Sponsors takes away that burden from the individual investor and manages for the highest and best total return."

"Many times, we find that the income we create using the DST exceeds the income the investor was creating on their own. In addition, the quality of the property, location and tenants almost always exceeds the relinquished property. DST owners are participating in properties that they, in most cases, could never have dreamed of investing in on their own. Another client I was working with had a profitable operating company that included a large portion of real estate in the operations. In his early 60's he had a heart attack and began to realize that the grind of running the business was taking a toll. While selling the business we were able to allocate a significant portion of the sales price to the real estate assets involved. This allowed us to take the maximum amount possible into a 1031 exchange.

"While he paid some taxes on the business portion of the transaction the bulk of the proceeds were able to be invested into a DST. That DST ended up creating more income than he was traditionally able to draw from his operating company. Another great example of putting the assets to work for you. Through proper planning the allocation of the sale price reduced his tax bill to the lowest possible level while providing the highest possible DST income going forward.

"In the end, most 1031 exchanges into DSTs that I have worked on over my career have:

1. Enhanced the Investors Income
2. Heightened the level of property owned
3. Improved the quality of life for investors
4. Simplified Tax returns
5. Reduced overall risk
6. Provided Greater Diversification
7. Assured income will continue after the primary real estate owner has passed on, whereby he has now maximized his tax deferral for good! Yes. It's nice!"

SHOULD I BUY MY OWN NNN OR A DST?

A retired University of California-San Diego economics professor recently told me that if he knew then what he knows now, he would certainly have put his $2 million investment in DSTs. He was interested in purchasing a triple net property (NNN, one in which the tenant or lessee agrees to pay maintenance, taxes and insurance), specifically a Kentucky Fried Chicken franchise.

The professor spent hours making a detailed analysis of 40 different KFCs. He even ventured to South Carolina to visit the property in which he was most interested. He went through the process of buying the property and financing part of the purchase. Six months later, he returned to the property and was disillusioned. He determined that an individual cannot buy a property with the kind of quality that a larger institution can purchase. He called his own purchase a "leftover," what remained after big REIT and DST purchases had been made.

He also bemoaned the kind of lease he had with the franchisee, which pales in comparison to corporate leases.

He told me, "When I think of all the work I did to get one percentage point higher cash flow than a DST, it just doesn't pencil out; the math just simply doesn't work. It would have taken me a couple hours to do the paperwork needed to do a DST and I would have been done with it."

ABOUT THE AUTHORS

DON MEREDITH is one of the early pioneers of the DST 1031 Exchange industry having identified the need and the benefits early on. He has been involved in placing his investors into hundreds of DST exchanges and continues to do so with passion and commitment. This entrepreneurial spirit and ability to adapt to a changing business environment undoubtedly came from his father and grandfather.

> "My father was an HR Manger and was always bringing home aptitude tests for me to take." His grandfather founded in 1939 a convention center that featured a seafood restaurant and inn catering to tourists and nearby Brunswick Naval Air Base, Bowdoin College, and BIW of Bath, Maine. And like his grandfather, he too had his own business.
>
> "While attending college, I started a cleaning and maintenance business which grew into airport/control tower contracts, ferry terminal, NBC and CBS buildings. The business took off and did really well. The business that I sold still exists today."

Over time Don wound up in the place he now calls home, San Diego. He has a background in money management with Paine Webber that was later acquired by the Swiss bank UBS. Don co-hosted a talk show on one of the prominent San Diego radio stations with a financial focus. Willing to try new things, which usually he becomes pretty good at, he took up oil pointing and stage acting after the age of 50. He is quite accomplished at both!

Don is past president and has been an active member of Rancho Santa Fe Rotary for over 21 years. He is also an active member, and on the Worship and Arts Commission of the Village Church at Rancho Santa Fe.

THOMAS KOSS has a wealth of experience in finance, investments and development primarily in commercial estate related fields. As an investment broker, a mortgage broker, mortgage banker and affordable housing consultant he has a broad-based understanding of most aspects of investment real estate.

Tom has owned and operated his own commercial real estate and finance companies for over 20 years. He holds a degree in economics from the University of Washington, is an avid reader of history and psychology, yachtsman, private pilot and a former ski school director.

Phone: 619.772.7738
tom@camrealtyadvisors.com

Made in United States
Orlando, FL
05 October 2022

23047239R00085